STUDIES IN AMERICAN HISTORY

VIII

ALEXANDER HAMILTON

AND THE BRITISH ORIENTATION OF AMERICAN FOREIGN POLICY, 1783-1803

BY

HELENE JOHNSON LOOZE

1969

MOUTON

THE HAGUE · PARIS

LIBRARY OF CONGRESS CATALOG CARD NUMBER: 68-17884

Printed in The Netherlands by Mouton & Co., Printers, The Hague.

My Mother

Elizabeth Johnstone Johnson

How can we hope for success in our European negotiations, if the nations of Europe have no confidence in the wisdom and vigor of the great Continental Government? This is the object on which their eyes are fixed; hence it is, America will derive its importance or insignificance in their estimation.

Hamilton to Governor Clinton,
February 13, 1778

We are laboring hard to establish in this country principles more and more *national* and free from all foreign ingredients, so that we may be neither 'Greeks nor Trojans,' but truly Americans.

Hamilton to Rufus King,
December 16, 1796

PREFACE

Respected historians have studied and evaluated the many accomplishments of Alexander Hamilton: as an economist of great perception, as a notable politician, as an intellect, and as a man whose human frailties were newsworthy. The purpose of this study is to investigate Hamilton as a diplomatic statesman, especially in regard to Great Britain and the period 1783-1803.

In the past some students and historians have called Hamilton the epitome of a quisling, while others found him jumping to ill-fated conclusions in the area of diplomacy. The following pages should satisfactorily deny either charge, for to Hamilton the primary incentive behind any American action — economic, diplomatic, or political — was establishment of a strong national state. Toward this end his performance was generally impeccable, even more particularly when Hamilton's own judgement and moral standards are the measure of evaluation.

I have found that Hamilton's true contributions to the diplomatic thought of his period and to the future course of United States foreign policy are expressed most fully in the more commonly recognized sources of Hamiltonian material. *The Works of Alexander Hamilton,* edited by Henry Cabot Lodge, have therefore furnished the fundamental material for this study. Hamilton's cabinet papers have proved invaluable, as they reveal the patterns of his logic and rationale more clearly than do his private letter records, except in the cases where he served in an advisory capacity on matters of national importance.

The first portion of my study is designed to present the basic concepts of the Hamiltonian dialectic bearing on relations between states, and the best course to be pursued by the United States in these interrelations. With this in mind, the major portion of the study is a careful exposition of the actual events in British-American relations between 1783 and 1803, and Hamilton's role in these. As American foreign policy was not solely concerned with Great Britain during this period, it has been necessary to include pertinent relations between the United States and other nations; namely, with France. An evaluation of the animator of these events and their impact upon the historical perspective of the new nation, draw the study to a close.

TABLE OF CONTENTS

CHAPTER I

MOTIVATIONS AND MAKERS OF FOREIGN POLICY

Alexander Hamilton has on the whole been thoroughly recognized and praised for his contributions to the economic responsibility of the American government. He has been adequately credited for his understanding and definition of the powers of the Federal Constitution. One area in which he has not been sufficiently regarded is that of diplomatic thought. His contributions to this field are notable, both in methodology and principle.

The world today shares a vital concern for the diplomatic relations among nations, having come to realize the importance such understanding promotes. In Hamilton's day diplomacy and international politics were not considered as a discipline. They were necessary, yes, but hardly the scientific tradition they are today. Hamilton was probably unconscious of the philosophical and theoretical import of his diplomatic programs and policies. He did, nevertheless, consciously practice a uniform system of reasoning and logic in defining American international interests and guiding their progress from inception to culmination. In both method and practice he offers a case study for students of international relations in divining the theories and problems of foreign policy in a new nation.

Disciplinarians in the diplomatic field today ask such questions as: How does a country establish its foreign policy interests and objectives? By what means does it pursue these foreign policy objectives? How is foreign policy fashioned? What are the elements of foreign policy? Let us suppose for this study that there are two types of approaches to foreign policy. The ideological approach, which supposes the policies of states vis-à-vis the rest of the world suggests expressions of prevailing political, social, and religious beliefs — foreign policy as a by-product of domestic politics. The second approach may be considered analytical. In this view policy rests on multiple determinants such as the state's historic tradition, geographical location, national interest, and purposes and security needs. This last approach recognizes that objective requirements of the national interest place certain limits upon the statesman seeking to formulate foreign policy. Using these categories, we shall probably find that the Hamiltonian statesman falls into the latter or analytical approach.

One intangible factor existing in nations which must be either acknowledged, or at least considered probable is the national mind — interpreter of the national interest. What shall we suppose the national mind to be? Carlton Hayes has noted:

A fourth and final use of 'nationalism' is to denote a condition of mind among members of a nationality, perhaps already possessed of a national state, a condition of mind in which loyalty to the ideal or to the fact of one's national state is superior to all other loyalties and of which pride in one's nationality and belief in its intrinsic excellence and in its 'mission' are integral parts.[1]

Hans Kohn finds that "Nationalism is a state of mind, in which the supreme loyalty of the individual is felt to be due the nation-state." [2]

Since the nation and nationalism are coincidental, their interests should be and probably are identical. The national mind is vague and so its interests will probably be ambiguous and difficult to define. One factor may be expected, however: the interests will generally be selfishly motivated. "It is true that communities are selfish, cannot help being selfish, and cannot be blamed for being selfish, since the human world is what it is." [3]

The task of the formulator of foreign policy then is to determine the hierarchy of national interests. What hope can national interest give us for interpreting the vagaries of foreign policy? It should help us, for it suggests the necessary and basic characteristic of any foreign policy, i.e., an adaptable, flexible nature.

The problem here becomes the actual formulation of foreign policy, or, from what source did the Hamiltonian foreign policy rationale spring? We have thus far avoided admitting that man is possibly not always selfishly motivated by his own interests but is perhaps impelled in his choices by his basically good nature. We must ask the question: will the national interest always be selfish by nature? Or

[1] Carlton Hayes, *Essays on Nationalism* (New York, The MacMillan Co., 1926), 6.
[2] Hans Kohn, *Nationalism: Its Meaning and History* (Princeton, C. Van Nostrand Co., 1955), 9.
[3] Raymond Aron, "The Quest for a Philosophy of Foreign Affairs", *Revue Française de Science Politique*, III (Jan.-March, 1953), 77.

is there another point from which foreign policy stems? Let us view the problem as a spiral of moving circles. The inner circle will be equated with nationalism and/or national interest, and the outermost circle will be equated with an international community and/or a utopian world. Does the formulation of foreign policy start with the national interest for Hamilton, or does it start from the assumption of the hope for or belief in an international community? If the framing of foreign policy is guided by national interest (the inner circle), does the movement of the spiral outwardly mean that international community will be achieved? Logically, it will not follow that national interest will become international interest, unless they are the same.

Let us equate the outside circle (an international community) with the basic goodness of man. If Hamilton assumed that man and his social nature are basically good and the circles are spiralling inwardly, would the outside circles change the selfish nature of the national interest? The facts of reality and science find any spiral action moves naturally from small to large and only by unnaturally induced energy from larger to smaller. The analogy suggests that national interest can more naturally become international community interest than can international community become nationalism. The solution to the mystery should be to find interests held in common by both ends of the spiral, unless, of course, the circles are concentric! Shall we find Hamilton's concept of the purposes of foreign policy energized from the center of the spiral or from the outside? Was his viewpoint that of the nationalist or the internationalist? Were his decisions on formulating foreign policy induced by matters of domestic national security? Did he envision the United States as a powerful nation among nations? Or did he foresee the United States as the hope of a utopian future?

We have only briefly glanced at the vast multitude of facets to be explored in the problems of foreign policy and its ultimate purposes. An integral part of foreign policy is diplomacy. Diplomacy is the means by which foreign policy is practiced. Diplomacy is not only the framing of policy, but rather its execution. It is the most effective means for accommodation between state relations that are sometimes in harmony but other times in conflict. Diplomacy requires an intimate knowledge of the mechanics of negotiation, endless patience, and consummate skill in adjusting national proposals without sacrificing vital objectives. Diplomacy becomes the vehicle of communi-

cation between nations. We shall see that Hamilton actively participated in the art of diplomacy.

In the formulation of foreign policy and diplomacy decisions must
be made. Who are the decision-makers? How do they define their
situations? The decision-makers are those on whom the responsibility
for forming and enforcing decisions falls. In every situation the decision-maker finds various things wanted and several courses of action
open by which to achieve these goals. Decision-making as a process
has received close study in recent years. It is a limited behavioral
approach to the greater study of international politics, but its discipline can well serve our purposes in examining Alexander Hamilton.

Hamilton had a clearly defined concept of the decision-maker's
role and the powers and responsibility which executive authority
implied. The sense of the community in the republican principle
governed the conduct of those to whom the community entrusted
the management of their affairs. This did not, however, said Hamilton, require unqualified compliance to every breeze of passion or
transient impulse which the people received from the arts of men
who flattered their prejudices to betray their interests.

When occasions present themselves, in which the interests of the people
are at variance with their inclinations, it is the duty of the persons whom
they have appointed to be the guardians of those interests to withstand
the temporary delusion, in order to give them time and opportunity for
more cool and sedate reflection.[4]

It was highly desirable that the executive should be in a situation to
dare to act on his own opinion with vigor and decision. Every power
vested in government was in its nature sovereign and included,
therefore, a right to employ all the means requisite and applicable
to the attainment of the ends of that power. Only restrictions and
exceptions specified in the Constitution, and immoral and contrary
means were limiting.[5] National exigencies could be provided for and
national inconveniences obviated by means of infinite variety, extent,
and complexity. There must, out of necessity then, be great latitude
of discretion in the selection and application of those means. "Hence,
consequently, the necessity and propriety of exercising the authorities

---

[4]   Henry Lodge (ed.), *The Federalist* (New York, G. P. Putnam's Sons, 1882),
446-47. Hereafter cited: Lodge, *Federalist*.
[5]   Hamilton to Washington, Feb. 23, 1791. Henry Lodge (ed.), *The Works of
Alexander Hamilton* (New York, G. P. Putnam's Sons, 1904), III, 446. Hereafter
cited: Lodge, *Works*.

intrusted to a government on principles of liberal construction." [6]

The liberal construction of means to provide for national exigencies granted Hamilton considerable administrative interpretation. Every power requisite to the full accomplishment of the objects committed to its care ought to be contained in a government, he thought. To execute the trusts for which it was responsible, it ought to be free from every control other than regard for the public good and a sense of public opinion. The superintendence of the national defense and public peace from foreign and domestic violence could not be assigned limits according to Hamilton. No other bounds than the exigencies of the nation and the resources of the community should be known. And, he concluded:

As revenue is the essential engine by which the means of answering the national exigencies must be procured, the power of procuring that article in its full extent must necessarily comprehend in that of providing for those exigencies.[7]

The basic component of the decision-making process to be kept in mind is the nature of choice; choices are in the final analysis made by the decision-maker. The occasion for decision arises from uncertainty; "choice involves valuation and evaluation in terms of a frame of reference".[8] Some aspects of the situation can no longer be taken for granted. Decision-makers have preferences, and the key questions here are: what is the nature of these preferences? What are the factors influencing them? "Information is selectively perceived and evaluated in terms of the decision-maker's frame of reference. Choices are made on the basis of preferences which are in part situationally and in part biographically determined." [9]

Hamilton's choices in guiding American foreign policy were influenced by the situation or existing circumstances, the means available for accomplishment, and the goals to be accomplished. In making the decisions, he drew from biographical (knowledge gained by study and experience) and situational (existing conditions or circumstances, both internal and external) preferences. Every decision is influenced in some measure by various criteria, and Hamilton's decisions or choices were no exception. The biographical basis for his preferences

[6] Lodge, *Works*, 455.
[7] Lodge, *Federalist*, 182.
[8] Richard Snyder, H. W. Bruck, and Burton Sapin, *Decision-Making as an Approach to the Study of International Politics* (Princeton, Princeton University Press, 1954), 65.
[9] *Ibid.*, 120.

will hold our attention first. The situational will fall into the context of the discourse.

As one reads the Greek and Roman authors, he is struck by the similar principles of logical reasoning and likeness of events between Hamilton's day and the men and circumstances of old. Hamilton must have been struck by this too, for his understanding and solutions to problems were in a marked degree like those of many centuries before. His grasp of their solutions and failures very probably aided his decisional choices. It is impossible to support this assumption except in a very general way. Hamilton read the classics, but which ones cannot be adequately stated as there is no record beyond mention of Demosthenes and Plutarch in his writings.[10] We know that he usually used Greek and Roman names for the signatures on his many printed articles and essays. Since it would be an impossibility to prove any direct connection, we shall only note that there is a marked resemblance between the solutions Hamilton found for American foreign relations and those which Thucydides reported in *The Peloponnesian War*.

Let us look at several examples to investigate this assumption. When the Corinthians, allies of the Lacedaemonians, came to Lacedaemon urging war against Athens, certain Athenians present rose to recommend quiet considerations. Their words are almost an exact duplicate of Hamilton's reasoning regarding Anglo-American relations.

Take time then in forming your resolution, as the matter is of great importance; and *do not be persuaded by the opinions and complaints of others to bring trouble on yourselves*, but *consider the vast influence of accident in war*, before you are engaged in it. As it continues, it *generally becomes an affair of chances*, chances from which neither of us is exempt, and whose event we must risk in the dark. *It is a common mistake in going to war to begin at the wrong end, to act first, and wait for disaster to discuss the matter.* But we are not yet by any means so misguided, nor, so far as we can see, are you; accordingly, while it is still open to us both to choose aright, we bid you not to dissolve the treaty, or to break your oaths, but to have our differences settled by arbitration according to our agreement.[11]

The Lacedaemonians were, nevertheless, led to the conclusion that Athens was openly aggressive and war must be declared at once.

[10]   I refer to notes taken by Hamilton from Demosthenes' Orations and Plutarch's Lives as found in the "Pay Book of the State Company of Artillery", 1777. Harold Syrett (ed.), *The Papers of Alexander Hamilton* (New York, Columbia University Press, 1961), I, 390-407.

[11]   Italics are not in the original but were added for emphasis.

Their king came forward and made a speech in which he described almost perfectly the conditions existing between Britain and America and the policy Hamilton followed to achieve Jay's Treaty.

For unless we can either beat them at sea, or deprive them of the revenues which feed their many, we shall meet with little but disaster. ... but I do bid you not to take up arms at once, but to send and remonstrate with them in a tone not too suggestive of war, nor again too suggestive of submission, and to employ the interval in perfecting our own preparations. ... war is a matter not so much of arms as money, which makes arms of use. *And this is more than ever true in a struggle between a continental and a maritime power.* ... but are taught to consider that the schemes of our enemies are not dissimilar to our own, and that the freaks of chance are not determinable by calculation. In practice we always base our preparations against an enemy on the assumption that his plans are good; indeed, it is right to rest our hopes not on a belief in in his blunders, but on the soundness of our provisions.

When the Athenian assembly discussed putting the Mitylenians to death for revolting, Diodotus spoke in the following way:

I think the two things most opposed to good counsel are haste and passion; haste usually goes hand in hand with folly, passion with coarseness and narrowness of mind. ... especially as we, your advisors, are responsible, while you, our audience, are not so. For if those who gave the advice, and those who took it, suffered equally, you would judge more calmly. ... *the question before us as sensible men is not their guilt, but our interests ...* but we are not in a court of justice, but in a political assembly; *and the question is not justice, but how to make the Mitylenians useful to Athens.* ... *I consider it far more useful for the preservation of our empire voluntarily to put up with injustice, than to put to death, however justly, those whom it is our interest to keep alive.*

These words are very similar to Hamilton's when he discussed the Nootka Sound controversy and American treaty obligations with France. The United States, Hamilton felt, should not lose sight of the real purposes of independence and eventual national security. Spitefully refusing British passage through United States territory and joining France in a war against all of Europe would be taking action denying the real interests of the United States, Hamilton maintained. Emphasis on the usefulness of the Mitylenians to the Athenians recommends to us also Hamilton's attraction to Britain. Diodotus wondered why they should put to death those whom it was in their interest to keep alive. Hamilton wondered why the United States should rebuff Great Britain when she could be so useful to the United States.

At the Melian Conference "disgrace" was considered:

You will surely not be caught by *that idea of disgrace,* which endangers that are disgraceful, and at the same time too plain to be mistaken, *proves so fatal to mankind;* since in too many cases the very men that have their eyes perfectly open to what they are rushing into, let the thing called disgrace, by the mere influence of a seductive name, lead them on to a point at which they become so *enslaved by the phrase as in fact to fall wilfully into hopeless disaster, and incur disgrace more disgraceful as the companion of error, than when it comes* as the result of misfortune.

Hamilton understood this sentiment with its weaknesses, and gave it no room when he viewed our association with Britain and France. He continually warned his fellow men that sentiments of passion and disgrace were to be felt only reservedly as they tended to blind right actions to simple reaction.

The Athenians proposed to conquer Sicily and they chose Nicias to lead the expedition. He did not approve of the plan and told his countrymen the same things that Hamilton did when the United States continued to violate the Treaty of 1783 and threaten war with Great Britain.

I affirm, then, that *you leave many enemies behind you here to go yonder and bring more back with you.* You imagine, perhaps, that the treaty which you have made can be trusted; *a treaty that will continue to exist nominally, as long as you keep quiet* — for nominal it has become, owing to the practices of certain men here and at Sparta — *but which in the event of a serious reverse in any quarter would not delay our enemies a moment in attacking us;* first, because the convention was forced upon them by disaster and was *less honorable to them than to us;* and secondly, because *in this very convention there are many points that are still disputed.* . . . and it is only too probable that *if they found our power divided,* as we are hurrying to do it, *they would attack us vigorously.* . . . A man ought, therefore, to consider these points, and *not to think of running risks with a country placed so critically, or of grasping at another empire before* we have secured the one we have already. . . .[12]

The Athenian conquest of Sicily failed miserably, it can be noted.

The words of Cicero, Demosthenes and Aristotle suggest a profound influence on Hamilton's thinking, although their influence, as Thucydides', can only be postulated. On moral duties, Cicero offers a foundation for Hamilton's rationalization of contract obligations and national interest. Cicero noted that:

[12] All the quotations are found in: Thucydides, *The Complete Writings of Thucydides: The Peloponnesian War* (New York, Random House, 1934), 45-8, 167-72.

... there are many occasions when actions that appear eminently worthy of the just man or the good man, as commonly say, change their complexion and present a different aspect. *It may at times be just not to return what is entrusted to our care, not to keep a promise, or to violate the laws of veracity and honour.* In such cases we should go back to the principles which I laid down at the outset, as the foundations of justice: do evil to no man; work for the common good. *When these principles are modified by circumstances, our duty likewise changes and is not fixed and invariable. Thus the fulfillment of a promise or agreement may be prejudicial either to him to whom it was made or to him who made it.*

In national affairs, Cicero recommended much the same as had Thucydides — war was a last resort.

In national affairs the laws of war must be strictly observed. There are two methods of settling a dispute, discussion and force; the one is characteristic of man, the other of beasts; *it is only when we cannot employ conciliation that we are justified in resorting to force.* Our one object in making war should be that we may live in peace unmolested; when victory is gained we should spare those who have not been cruel or barbarous.[13]

The obligations and rights of statesmen were considered by Demosthenes in his First Philippic: "... that just as a general may be expected to lead his armies, so are men of prudent counsel to guide circumstances, in order that their resolutions may be accomplished, not their motions determined by the events." [14] We know (from notes in his Pay Book) that Hamilton read these orations. It is legitimate to assume that he accepted the analysis as valid. He became one of its most ardent practitioners.

Aristotle listed three qualifications "required of those who are to fill the highest offices: (1) first of all, *loyalty to the established constitution*; (2) *great administrative capacity*; (3) *virtue and justice of the kind proper to the particular form of government.*" [15] The first of these Hamilton certainly adopted, for once the new Constitution was written, he became one of its loyal supporters. The second and third qualifications he recommended for executive responsibility and authority in the American government, for the president as well as for himself. The impact of these selected quotations upon Hamiltonian thought and action will become even more apparent as we progress, for they are incorporated in his dialectics and planning.

[13] Cicero, *The Basic Works of Cicero* (New York, Random House, 1951), 15.
[14] Demosthenes, *The Crown, the Philippics and Ten Other Orations of Demosthenes* (New York, E. P. Dutton & Co., 1923).
[15] Aristotle, *On Man in the Universe: Metaphysics, Parts of Animals, Ethics, Politics, Poetics* (New York, Walter J. Black, Inc., 1943), 363.

CHAPTER II

FIVE HAMILTONIAN PREMISES

The Hamiltonian dialectic offers recurring themes responsive to the events between 1783 and 1803. They are five: peace, interest, neutrality, negotiation, and obligation of contract. These ideas, once set forth, will facilitate a better understanding of Hamilton's foreign policy and its British orientation.

Perhaps the most constant of these is "peace".[1] Peace, he said, was the greatest interest of this country in its external relations. Any commercial advantages we acquired by particular treaties were of far less moment than peace itself. For, with peace, "the force of circumstances will enable us to make our way sufficiently fast in trade".[2] War would seriously wound our growth and prosperity. He thought that if we could escape it for ten or twelve years more, we might "then meet it without much inquietude, and could advance with energy and effect any pretensions to greater commercial advantages which we sought".[3]

The preservation of peace was of primary concern for the future of the United States. Peace meant that the United States could hope to enjoy the greatness of her potential. As yet her stature as a nation was meager, but with time and effort, her future was unlimited.

'PEACE, in the particular situation of this independent country, is an object of such GREAT and PRIMARY magnitude, that it ought not to be relinquished unless the relinquishment be clearly necessary to PRESERVE OUR HONOR in some UNEQUIVOCAL point, or to avoid the sacrifice of some RIGHT or INTEREST of MATERIAL and PERMANENT importance.' This is the touchstone of every question which can come before us respecting our foreign concerns.[4]

---

[1] Hammond, the British Minister in the United States, wrote that: "... all his [Hamilton's] interests political and personal are so implicated in the preservation of peace as to leave me no doubt of his sincerity." Hammond to Lord Grenville, April 2, 1793. F.O. 5:1, No. 11. Lib. Cong.

[2] Hamilton to Washington, Cabinet Papers, July 9, 1795. Lodge, *Works*, V, 176-77.

[3] Lodge, *Works*, 177.

[4] "Camillus", 1795. Lodge, *Works*, V, 235.

The United States was not in a position effectively to prosecute offensive war, said Hamilton, or for that matter even defensive war. "The U. States have the strongest motives to avoid war. They may lose a great deal; they can gain nothing. They may be annoyed much and can annoy comparatively little." [5] Powerful states could frequently hazard a high and haughty tone with good policy. A weak state could never do it without imprudence. The United States was best described in the latter category, even though we were the embryo of a great empire. Hamilton thought it better suited our situation to measure each step with utmost caution, hazarding as little as possible in cases where we were injured. We should blend moderation with firmness and brandish the weapons of hostility only when their use was unavoidable.[6]

Hamilton enumerated the inducements for cultivating peace, of which few nations had stronger inducements than the United States. We were in an infant state and had no marine to protect our commerce. War would be a calamity as it would not only arrest America's present rapid progress to strength and prosperity, but would throw us back into a state of debility and impoverishment from which we would not re-emerge for years. "Our trade, navigation, and mercantile capital would be essentially destroyed", he concluded.[7]

Another essential theme in Hamilton's thinking is that of "interest". Interest is closely tied to almost all of his deductions, licensing the greater portion of his policy decisions. The interests of nations were the formulators of national policies, both nationally and internationally. The actions of nations "... have been ... under the control of the principles of self-interest, which ever have and ever will govern the affairs of nations".[8] Interest was selfish; its first consideration was for itself. "Nothing can be more erroneous, than the opinion that any nation is likely to yield up its own interest, in order, gratuitously, to advance that of another." [9] These were facts which must necessarily be recognized, or the actions of nations became inexplicable. Any nation would think first of its own interest in making decisions. "They [France] did then as we have done now, and as every discerning

[5]   Undated answer by Hamilton to the President's questions for McHenry. Bernard Steiner, *The Life and Correspondence of James McHenry* (Cleveland, The Burrows Bros. Co., 1907), 217.
[6]   "Camillus", 1795. Lodge, *Works*, V, 206.
[7]   *Ibid.*, 201-02.
[8]   Lodge, *Works*, VI, 8.
[9]   *Ibid.*

nation will do — they regarded only their own interest and advantage, and not that of any other nation." [10]

Interest was a fact in the relations among nations which, once admitted, could account for behavioral decisions, Hamilton explained. "The true question always is upon the collective merits of the instruments; whether, upon the whole, it reasonably accommodates the opinions and interests of the parties." [11] Interest, however, was not only reason, it was human.

Though nations, in the main, are governed by what they suppose their interest, he must be imperfectly versed in human nature who thinks it indifferent whether the maxims of a State tend to excite kind or unkind dispositions in others, or who does not know that these dispositions may insensibly mould or bias the views of self-interest. This were to suppose that rulers only reason — do not feel; in other words, are not men. [12]

The duty of a government and its rulers, Hamilton said, is to the interests of the nation or state; they must administer with those interests in mind. Individual benevolence, kindness, or passions, were emotions without place. Hamilton discussed this in reference to the use of good offices among nations. The predominant motive of good offices from one nation to another was the interest or advantage of the nation performing them, he began. The rule of morality in this respect was not the same between nations as between individuals.

The duty of making its own welfare the guide of its actions, is much stronger upon the former than upon the latter in proportion to the greater magnitude and importance of national compared with individual happiness, and to the greater permanency of the effects of national than of individual conduct. [13]

Millions of people and future generations were concerned in the measures of the government. The consequences of private actions by individuals ordinarily terminated with the individual or were circumscribed within a narrow compass. An individual could on numerous occasions indulge the emotions of generosity and benevolence, without an eye to or at the expense of his own interest. A government could rarely be justified in pursuing such a course. If it did, it should be confined within much stricter bounds. [14] Hamilton was not trying

---

[10] "The Answer", 1796. Lodge, *Works*, VII, 226.
[11] "Camillus", 1795. Lodge, *Works*, VI, 116.
[12] Lodge, *Works*, V, 453.
[13] "Pacificus", 1793. Lodge, *Works*, IV, 464-65.
[14] Footnote by Hamilton: "This conclusion derives confirmation from the reflection that under every form of government rulers are only trustees for the hap-

to recommend a selfish policy, but was endeavoring to show "that a policy regulated by their own interest, as far as justice and good faith permit, is, and ought to be, their prevailing one. . . ." [15] To ascribe to a different principle or deduce arguments for a self-denying and self-sacrificing gratitude by a nation receiving good offices from another, would be to misrepresent or misconceive what are usually the springs of national conduct.

Interest was, then, the factor which should guide the national conduct. What were the interests of the United States according to Hamilton?

. . . it is not the interest of the United States to be engaged in any war whatsoever. . . . We have acted right hitherto in laying it down as a principle, not to suffer ourselves to be drawn into the wars of Europe; and if we must have a war, I hope it will be for refusing to depart from that principle.[16]

Neutrality suited the interests of America in her present condition. "The neutral and the pacific policy appears to me to mark the true path to the United States." [17] She possessed potential but only power could enforce conformity and recognition, said Hamilton. "It seems evidently our true policy to cultivate neutrality. This, at least, is the ground on which we ought to stand, until we can see more of the scene, and can have secured the means of changing it with advantage." [18] However,

The rights of neutrality will only be respected when they are defended by an adequate power. A nation, despicable by its weakness, forfeits even the privilege of being neutral. Under a vigorous national government, the natural strength and resources of the country, directed by a common interest, would baffle all the combinations of European jealousy to restrain our growth.[19]

The United States could best build her strength by remaining peaceful, admonished Hamilton. Peace and neutrality were consanguine. Our great rule of conduct in regard to foreign nations ought to be to

---

piness and interest of their nation, and cannot, consistently with their trust, follow the suggestions of kindness and humanity toward others, to the prejudice of their constituents."
[15]   *Ibid.*, 465.
[16]   "The Answer", 1796. Lodge, *Works,* VII, 228.
[17]   Hamilton to Edward Carrington, May 26, 1792. Lodge, *Works,* IX, 528.
[18]   Hamilton to Washington, Cabinet Paper, Sept. 15, 1790. Lodge, *Works,* I, 334.
[19]   Lodge, *Federalist,* 63.

have as little political connection as possible with them. Europe had a set of primary interests which were remote, or more correctly, unlike ours. If the United States remained united, under an efficient government, Hamilton foretold that:

the period is not distant when we may defy material injury from external annoyance — when we may take such an attitude as will cause the neutrality we shall at any time resolve to observe, to be violated with caution — when it will be the interest of belligerent nations, under the impossibility of making acquisitions upon us, to be very careful how either forced us to throw our weight into the opposite scale — when we may choose peace or war, as our interest, guided by justice, shall dictate.[20]

American foreign policy should be flexible and facile Hamilton felt, so that its best interests could be served; if it were static it would atrophy. This theme is present in almost every strategy of Hamilton's. Permanent alliances with any part of the foreign world were to be avoided. But, he warned, it should not be "a general principle, to avoid permanent or close alliances. Taking care always to keep ourselves by suitable establishments in a respectably defensive position, we may safely trust to occasional alliances for extraordinary emergencies."[21]

America's interests were best served by moderate, thoughtful policies. The careful assessment of every situation would more often lead to satisfactory solutions, than would passionate reactions, encouraged Hamilton. Resentment and rage in a nation sometimes compelled governments to war, contrary to their own calculations of policy. A government did through passion what reason forbade when it participated in this propensity. The animosity of nations was made subservient to hostile projects which originated in ambition and sinister motives. As Hamilton noted, "The peace, often, and sometimes the liberty of nations, has been the victim of this cause."[22]

Since the future well-being and success of the United States rested upon the retention of peace, a foreign policy adjustable to change and capable of modification was implied. Conciliation and compromise were essential to such a program; negotiation the means of accomplishment.

Besides . . . in national controversies, it is of real importance to conciliate the good opinion of mankind; and it is even useful to preserve or gain that

---

[20] Hamilton's "Original Draft" of the Farewell Address, August 1796. Lodge, *Works*, VIII, 210-11.
[21] Lodge, *Works*, VIII, 210-11.
[22] *Ibid.*, 208.

of our enemy. The latter facilitates accommodation and peace; the former attracts good offices, friendly interventions, sometimes direct support, from others.[23]

In differences between the United States and other nations, Hamilton felt the United States should carefully avoid measures tending to widen any breach, and "scrupulously abstain from whatever may be construed into reprisals, till after the employment of all amicable means has reduced it to a certainty that there is no alternative".[24] In all disputes between nations

... where one party is not powerful enough to dictate to the other, and where there is a mutual disposition to avoid war, the natural retreat for both is in compromise, which waives the question of first aggression or delinquency. This is the salve for national pride; the escape for mutual error; the bridge by which nations, arrayed against each other, are enabled to retire with honor, and without bloodshed, from the field of contest. ... What sensible man, what humane man, will deny that a compromise, which secures substantially the objects of interest, is always preferable to war....[25]

The infliction of injuries by one nation upon another were causes of war, he said. If a nation meant to negotiate before going to war, it should prepare for war and proceed to negotiate, avoiding reprisals till the issue of the negotiation. This was the "course of moderation, propriety, and wisdom".[26]

In Hamilton's thinking negotiation was the preferred course of action, but it was inconceivable that negotiation would not be accompanied by preparation for war. We should be in a respectable military posture, for war could come upon us whether we chose it or not. When we were able to defend ourselves and annoy those who attacked us, we would have established the best method of securing our peace. "The pains taken to preserve peace, include a proportional responsibility that equal pains be taken to be prepared for war." [27] It was the duty of a government to take all possible chances of avoiding war. Negotiation gained time for defensive preparations in case of unreconcilable differences. Furthermore, it could dispose the adversary to reasonable accommodation. Hamilton summarized his viewpoint in 1797: "... pacify by negotiation, vigorous preparation

23 "Camillus", 1795. Lodge, *Works*, V, 452.
24 *Ibid.*, 206.
25 *Ibid.*, 213.
26 Hamilton to Washington, Cabinet Paper, April 14, 1794. Lodge, *Works*, V, 106.
27 Hamilton to Washington, March 8, 1794. Lodge, *Works*, X, 63, 65.

for war, and defensive measures with regard to our trade. . . ." [28]

Acts of reprisal against another nation were rarely effective or useful, Hamilton insisted, for

the passions of men stifle calculation. . . . the actual experiment of an exercise of the pretended right, by way of reprisal for an injury complained of, would commonly be as inefficacious as the menace of it to arrest general hostilities. Pride is roused; resentment kindled; and where there is even no disposition to those hostilities, the probability is that they follow. Nations, like individuals, ill brook the idea of receding from their pretensions under the rod, or of admitting the justice of an act of retaliation of reprisal by submitting to it. [29]

On another occasion, he said: "But acts of reprisal speak a contrary effect — they change negotiation into peremptory demand, and they brandish a rod over the party on whom the demand is made. He must be humble indeed, if he comply with the demand to avoid the stripe." [30]

Hamilton best explained his concept of obligation to contracts during the controversy over the French Alliance of 1778. The key term around which he built his arguments was "gratitude" and its relationship to obligation. A forecast of his mature opinion came in the Nootka Sound question. He founded a portion of his argument upon his concept of gratitude. The very sound of the word gratitude imposed respect, he said, and wherever even the appearance of a claim was founded, it was not a pleasing task to dispute it. "But where a word may become the basis of a political system, affecting the essential interests of the state, it is incumbent upon these who have any concern in the public administration, to appreciate its true import and application." [31] Even though painful to admit, Hamilton insisted that any reflection on gratitude would make it a duty, a sentiment, which between nations rarely had any solid foundation.

Faith and justice between nations were obligations precise and determinate. "But by exaggerating them, or giving them a fanciful extension, they would be in danger of losing their just force. This would be converting them into fetters, which a nation would ere long become impatient to break, as consistent neither with its prosperity nor its safety." [32] Hamilton emphasized the obligations of faith

[28]   Hamilton to Rufus King, April 8, 1797. Lodge, *Works*, 255.
[29]   "Camillus", 1795. Lodge, *Works*, V, 444.
[30]   Hamilton to Washington, Cabinet Paper, April 14, 1794. *Ibid.*, 106.
[31]   Hamilton to Washington, Cabinet Paper, Sept. 15, 1790. Lodge, *Works*, I, 321-22.
[32]   *Ibid.*, 325.

and justice as absolute and their utility as unquestionable; their relation to objects was generally brought within clear and intelligible rules. The same could not be said for gratitude. Not very often could a solid foundation for sentiment be found between nations. A question of even greater difficulty, was how far sentiment might justifiably be permitted to operate. The basis of gratitude was a benefit received or intended, originating in a regard to the interest of the party to whom the benefit was conferred. "If a service is rendered from views relative to the immediate interest of the party who performs it, and is productive of reciprocal advantages, there seems scarcely, in such a case, to be an adequate basis for a sentiment like that of gratitude." [33] Gratitude, as far as Hamilton was concerned, could even exact a sacrifice of the interest of the obligated party.

At another time, Hamilton again used gratitude as a rationale. "Gratitude", he said, "is due for favors received; and this virtue may exist among nations as well as among individuals; but the motive of the benefit must be solely the advantage of the party on whom it was conferred, else it ceases to be a favor." [34]

Obligation of contract and the sentiment of gratitude were not analogous to Hamilton. Gratitude was not the central factor to be considered in questions of obligation. Instead, "all contracts are to receive a reasonable construction. Self-preservation is the first duty of a nation. . . ." [35] Gratitude was an uncertain and precarious element, one which depended not upon reason but upon sentiment and feeling. These were not valid foundations for judging. Mutual interest and reciprocal advantage should be the criteria. These are the significant premises in the Hamiltonian concept of obligation.

Hamilton, as Horatius, well summarized his recommendations for the general framework of American foreign policy.

Reason, religion, philosophy, policy, disavow the spurious and odious doctrine, that we ought to cherish and cultivate enmity with any nation whatever.

In reference to a nation with whom we have such extensive relations of commerce as with Great Britain — to a power so capable, from her maritime strength, of annoying us — it must be the offspring of treachery or extreme folly. If you consult your true interest your motto cannot fail to be: 'PEACE and TRADE with ALL NATIONS: beyond our present engagements, POLITICAL CONNECTION with NONE.' [36]

---

[33]   "Pacificus", 1793. Lodge, *Works,* IV, 463-64.
[34]   "The Answer", 1796. Lodge, *Works,* VII, 226-27.
[35]   "Pacificus", 1793. Lodge, *Works,* IV, 457.
[36]   "Horatious", May 1795. Lodge, *Works,* V, 184.

CHAPTER III

INTERNATIONAL RESPECT

Commercial intercourse, national independence and international respect are interdependent in the Hamiltonian logic. Their mutually dependent nature could operate at optimum once the political nature of men and nations was known and used, Hamilton claimed. It was important to recognize the principles of human behavior as they existed in fact, rather than in theory. "... the passions of human nature are abundant sources of contention and hostility", he said.[1] It had invariably been found that monetary passions and immediate interests had a more active and imperious control over human conduct than had general or remote considerations of policy, utility or justice. Hamilton wanted the nation to awake from the deceitful dream of a golden age and adopt as a practical maxim for the direction of our political conduct the thesis that we and the rest of the world were yet far from the happy empire of perfect wisdom and virtue.[2]

Because of the jealousies, power drives, and ambition for conquest among nations, wars would probably always exist, Hamilton presumed. "Perpetual peace will not exist." [3]

To judge from the history of mankind, we shall be compelled to conclude that the fiery and destructive passions of war reign in the human breast with much more powerful sway than the mild and beneficent sentiments of peace; and that to model our political systems upon speculations of lasting tranquility, is to calculate on the weaker springs of the human character.[4]

While war was virtually inevitable, the isolated situation of the United States gave her the hope of avoiding clashes with other nations. "Our detached and distant situation invites us to a different course, and

[1] Hamilton to Governor Clinton, Oct. 3, 1783. Lodge, *Works*, IX, 394.
[2] Lodge, *Federalist*, 28, 32.
[3] Hamilton to Gouverneur Morris, Jan. 10, 1801. Lodge, *Works*, X, 410.
[4] Lodge, *Federalist*, 197.

enables us to pursue it."[5] Hamilton admonished, however, that the United States must not depend upon her preferred geographic position as a safeguard for her security. Though the Atlantic Ocean separated the United States from Europe, various considerations warned us against excesses of confidence or security. Stretching far into our rear, he said, were growing settlements subject to British dominion. Colonies and establishments subject to Spain extended to meet the British settlements. This situation, plus the vicinity of the West Indian Islands, which belonged to the British and Spanish, created between them and us a common interest. The savage tribes on our western frontier should be regarded as our natural enemies because they had most to fear from us. The Indians were the natural allies of Britain and Spain, he said, because they had most to hope from them. Navigational and communication improvements had rendered distant nations neighbors, and Britain and Spain were among the principal maritime powers of Europe. A concert between those two nations in the future was not improbable, he thought, for every day the consanguinity between France and Spain was diminishing. Politicians had always, Hamilton commented, "with great reason considered the ties of blood as feeble and precarious links of political connection".[6] These combinations of circumstances admonished us not to be too sanguine in considering America out of the reach of danger.

For the United States and every nation, Hamilton said,

Safety from external danger is the most powerful director of national conduct. ... The violent destruction of life and property incident to war, the continual effort and alarm attendant on a state of continual danger, will, compel nations the most attached to liberty to resort for repose and security to institutions which have a tendency to destroy their civil and political rights. To be more safe, they at length become willing to run the risk of being less free.[7]

What were the chief sources of expense in government, Hamilton asked? Wars and rebellions, he thought.

The expenses arising from those institutions which are lucrative [sic] to the mere domestic policy of a state, to the support of its legislative, executive, and judicial department, with their different appendage, and to the encouragement of agriculture and manufactures ... are insignificant in comparison with those which relate to the national defense.[8]

[5] *Ibid.*, 41.
[6] *Ibid.*, 144-45.
[7] *Ibid.*, 41.
[8] *Ibid.*, 198.

It must be admitted that a nation needed an adequate defense against offensive measures, but the costs of war were prohibitive for the economy of even a well-established nation. In Great Britain fourteen-fifteenths of the annual income "are absorbed in the payment of the interest of debts contracted for carrying on wars in which that country has been engaged, and in the maintenance of fleets and armies".[9] Would a new nation then do well to contract debts from wars before its own security and efficient government were firmly stabilized? To do so was utter folly Hamilton intoned.

Peace and war would not always be left to the option of the United States; she could not count on moderation or hope to extinguish the ambition of others. The United States would, indeed, have to see her own security. To accomplish this, Hamilton insisted, she must retain her peace. Moreover, she ought to stay out of the reach of foreign entanglements. But complete isolation would not answer all the necessities demanded by a growing nation. The United States would have to participate in the normal channels of intercourse between nations. Harmony, liberal intercourse, and commerce with all nations was recommended by justice, humanity, and interest, said Hamilton. America's commercial policy should neither seek nor grant exclusive favors or preference, but should hold an equal hand, while consulting the natural course of things. We should diffuse and diversify by gentle means the streams of commerce, but force nothing — "establishing with powers so disposed temporary rules of intercourse, the best that present circumstances and mutual opinion of interest will permit, but temporary, and liable to be abandoned or varied, as time, experience and future circumstances dictate...."[10] It was folly for one nation to expect disinterested favor from another, and to accept favors was to part with a portion of its independence. A nation might well find itself in the condition of having given equivalents for nominal favors and being reproached with ingratitude in the bargain. "There can be no greater error in national policy than to desire, expect, or calculate upon real favors."[11]

The crucial point from which national independence and international respect took their importance was a thriving commerce in Hamilton's plan.

---

[9] *Ibid.*
[10] Hamilton, "Original Draft" of the Farewell Address, Aug. 1796. Lodge, *Works*, VIII, 211-12.
[11] *Ibid.*, 212.

The prosperity of commerce is ... the most useful as well as the most productive source of national wealth. ... A nation cannot long exist without revenues. Destitute of this essential support, it must resign its independence, and sink into the degraded condition of a province. ... Revenue, therefore, must be had at all events.[12]

Commerce, it is manifest, like any other object of enterprise or industry, will prosper in proportion as it is secure. Its security, consequently, promoting its prosperity, extends its advantages. Security is indeed essential to its having a due and regular course.[13]

... power without revenue, in political society, is a name.[14]

Money is, with propriety, considered as the vital principle of the body politic; as that which sustains its life and motion, and enables it to perform its most essential functions.[15]

The success of the United States or any state rested upon its national wealth. Hamilton considered this principle vital. A prosperous commerce was the most useful and productive source of such wealth. As commerce flourished, land value rose proportionally. How could it happen otherwise, he asked.

Could that which procures a freer vent for the products of the earth, which furnishes new incitements to the cultivation of land, which is the most powerful instrument in increasing the quantity of money in a state — could that, in fine, which is the faithful handmaid of labor and industry, in every shape, fail to augment that article which is the prolific parent of far the greatest part of the objects upon which they are exerted?[16]

The ability of a country to pay taxes was proportional to the quantity of money in circulation and to the celerity with which it circulated. "Commerce, contributing to both these objects, must of necessity render the payment of taxes easier, and facilitate the requisite supplies to the treasury." [17] It was obvious after reviewing the state of the country, the habits of the people, and experiences of the past that it was impracticable to raise any considerable sum by direct taxation. The United States would for a long time have to rely for the means of revenue chiefly on duties. "In this country", Hamilton stated, "if the principal part [of revenue] be not drawn from com-

[12]   Lodge, *Federalist*, 67, 72.
[13]   "Camillus", 1795. Lodge, *Works*, V, 444.
[14]   "The Continentalist", 1781. Lodge, *Works*, I, 262.
[15]   Lodge, *Federalist*, 175.
[16]   *Ibid.*, 68.
[17]   *Ibid.*, 68.

merce, it must fall with oppressive weight upon land".[18] The advent
of such a policy would result in disunion.

The maritime powers of Europe looked with uneasiness upon the
commercial character of America. They were apprehensive that
America would interfere in the carrying trade which was the support
of navigation and foundation of naval strength among them. Hamilton surmised that the maritime powers would seek to foster divisions
among the states of America and deprive her of an active commerce
in her own bottoms. Such a policy would have answered the threefold purpose of preventing American interference in their navigation,
preventing us from monopolizing the profits of their trade, "and of
clipping the wings by which we might soar to a dangerous greatness".[19]

Hamilton believed that "one of the weak sides of republics . . . is
that they afford too easy an inlet to foreign corruption".[20] But if this
weakness could be countered by a strong united government, then
the United States might initiate prohibitory regulations which in
turn would oblige foreign countries to bid against each other for the
privileges of American markets. The importance of the markets of
three million people to any manufacturing nation would be obvious.
Let us suppose, he suggested, that the United States had a government capable of excluding Great Britain from all our ports. What
probable effect would this have upon American politics? It would
enable us to negotiate with a fair prospect of success, he thought, for
valuable and extensive commercial privileges in the British dominions. The disadvantage to Britain of such a state of things, aided by
the prepossession of a great part of Britain favoring American trade
and the importunities of the West Indies, would produce a relaxation
of her system. Britain would then let us into the markets of those
islands and elsewhere, from which American trade would derive
substantial benefits. While we could not expect to make such gains
without equivalent exemptions and immunities in American markets,
such a point having been made with the British government would
likely have a correspondent effect on the conduct of other nations.
They would not, Hamilton thought, be inclined "to see themselves
altogether supplanted in our trade".[21]

18   Ibid., 72.
19   Ibid., 60-1.
20   Ibid., 132.
21   Ibid., 61-2.

Another resource for influencing the conduct of Europe in this respect would arise from establishing a navy. "An active external commerce demands a naval power to protect it. . . ." [22] Naval strength would enable the United States to bargain with great advantage for commercial privileges. Moreover, "a price would be set not only upon our friendship, but upon our neutrality . . . we may hope, ere long, to become the arbiter of Europe in America, and to be able to incline the balance of European competition in this part of the world as our interest may dictate".[23]

Only a vigorous national government could achieve these ends. It may at times be forced to comply or compromise its immediate goals, but with time and the gaining of power, it would become better able to make its interests and demands felt. Through an active commerce the wealth and consequently the strength of a nation was built. These interests would lead it into and out of the most beneficial relationships for the United States. But, Hamilton admonished, "upon the whole, we shall be least likely to be deceived, by taking this as the basis of our commercial system, that we are not to make particular sacrifices to, nor expect particular favors from, any powers".[24]

With commerce underwriting the future strength of the national government, the commercial powers of the world were the partners Hamilton sought. Who were they? Great Britain, France, and Spain as the major maritime powers, and in a lesser degree their European neighbors. Of these, Britain and France were the more important. The American parent state had been Great Britain; their commercial ties were of two centuries standing. They shared a common language, and a mutually beneficial commercial intercourse. Hamilton was convinced that the United States received the greater commercial benefit from Britain. And, moreover, that British revenue gained much from the new American nation. Facts substantiate his conviction.[25]

As early as 1774 Hamilton wrote of the commercial benefits existing between Great Britain and her American colonies.

It is no easy matter to make any tolerably exact estimate of the advantages that accrue to Great Britain, Ireland, and the West Indies from their commercial intercourse with the colonies; nor, indeed, is it necessary.

---

[22] Draft by Hamilton of Washington's Speech to Congress, Dec. 7, 1796. Lodge, *Works*, VIII, 218-19.

[23] Lodge, *Federalist*, 63.

[24] Hamilton to Washington, Cabinet Paper, July 9, 1795. Lodge, *Works*, V, 180.

[25] See Bradford Perkins, *The First Rapprochement* (Philadelphia, University of Pennsylvania Press, 1955), 12-16.

Every man, the least acquainted with the state and extent of our trade, must be convinced it is the source of immense revenues to the parent state, and gives employment and bread to a vast number of his Majesty's subjects.[26]

A suspension of trade would cause beggary and wretchedness in Britain and the West Indies could not subsist without the United States, the youthful Hamilton continued.[27] If Britain attempted to cut off all external sources of trade "it would be extremely hurtful to the commerce of Great Britain to drive us to the necessity of laying a regular foundation for manufactures of our own, which, if once established, could not easily, if at all, be undermined or abolished". Furthermore, "it would be very expensive to the nation to maintain a fleet for the purpose of blocking up our ports and destroying our trade; nor could she interrupt our intercourse with foreign climes without, at the same time, retrenching her own revenues. . . ." [28]

These early convictions did not measurably change later, except to increase. Hamilton insisted that trade with Great Britain was more valuable to the revenue of the United States than our trade with France. He impressed this upon Washington, who noted to Jefferson, that "the Secretary of the Treasury has, more than once declared, and has offered to discuss and prove that we receive more substantial benefits . . . from British regulations with respect to the commerce of this Country than we do from those of France. . . ." [29]

A full discussion of this premise came in January 1794, in Hamilton's "View of the Commercial Regulations of France & Great Britain in reference to the United States".[30] "The commercial system of Great Britain makes no discriminations to the *prejudice* of the United States as *compared* with other foreign powers." [31] Instead, Britain's commer-

---

[26] "A Full Vindication", Dec. 15, 1774. Lodge, *Works*, I, 20.

[27] From 1783 on a whole series of amendments were necessary to provide for the sustenance of British North America and restrictions on the trade between the British West Indies and the United States were repeatedly relaxed to avoid famine. In practice the British trans-Atlantic possessions depended on the United States for supply, and as Great Britain became increasingly industrialized, she relied more and more on the American consumer. Gerald Graham, *Sea Power and British North America 1783-1820* (Cambridge, Harvard University Press, 1941), 275.

[28] "A Full Vindication", *op. cit.*, 30.

[29] Washington to The Secretary of State, Dec. 1, 1793. John Fitzpatrick (ed.), *The Writings of George Washington* (Washington, United States Government Printing Office, 1940), XXXIII, 162.

[30] Draft by Hamilton of Outline of Smiths' Speech on Madison's Resolutions of Jan. 3, 1794. Lodge, *Works*, V, 206-19.

[31] *Ibid.*, 206.

cial system made important discriminations in favor of the United States as compared with other nations. Tobacco, lumber, pot and pearl ash, tar and pitch, pig and bar iron, when carried from the United States to Britain were either exempt from duties or paid much less duty, giving the United States a clear advantage in the competition for the British market. American vessels in direct trade with Britain were in various instances exempted from duties, which were paid by ships of other nations. In general, American shipping in this trade was on the same footing with vessels of the British colonies. A variety of commodities was also admitted into the British West Indies, which were not given to similar commodities of other nations. "... the commercial system of Great Britain is more favorable and friendly to the United States than to other foreign countries." [32]

Continuing his opening general observations, Hamilton turned to France. Previous to the French Revolution, the French commercial system made fewer and less important discriminations favorable to the United States, as compared with other foreign nations, than that of Britain. Privileges in the West Indies were the same. Beyond the articles of fish oils, discriminations favorable to the United States in direct trade with France did not exist. There was ground to assert, Hamilton stated, "that the commercial system of France towards the United States as compared with other foreign nations, has been and now is less favorable and friendly than that of Great Britain." [33]

Hamilton examined in detail the commercial articles of the United States in their trade with Britain and France. As to flour, he found that it could "only be carried occasionally to Great Britain as well as to France, but the occasions have hitherto been more frequent in Great Britain than in France". [34] Flour could not be sent to France without loss, and prohibitory duties were laid against it by Britain. One quarter which interested the United States to have access to as a market for their flour, was the West India Islands. "Here the comparison is decidedly in favor of Great Britain. The general system of France is to prohibit the *reception* of our floor in her West India markets — that of Great Britain to *permit it.*" [35] It was true that there were occasional suspensions confined to "*cases of necessity*", but the

[32] Draft by Hamilton of Outline of Smiths' Speech on Madison's Resolutions of Jan. 3, 1795. Lodge, *Works*, IV, 207.
[33] *Ibid.*
[34] *Ibid.*, 208.
[35] *Ibid.*, 209.

French system which excluded the United States as far as possible could not be viewed any less favorably than suspension. "Flour appears to be the principal staple of the United States. This principal staple is, upon the whole, more favored by the regulations of Great Britain than of France." [36]

Neither Britain or France produced tobacco. Any duty, therefore, would fall upon the buyers and not the sellers. Prior to the French Revolution there was no import duty in France upon tobacco, but it was under a monopoly of the Farmers General. This situation destroyed free competition among purchasers and was far more disadvantageous to the United States than any tolerable duty. As of 1791 United States tobacco was on no better footing in France than in any other nation. In Britain a considerably higher duty was paid on foreign tobacco other than that of the United States, and it could be carried to Britain in United States vessels on the same terms as in British bottoms. The ships of other nations bringing tobacco were subject to a higher duty than the ships of Great Britain.

... in Great Britain a higher duty is charged on other foreign tobacco than upon ours; as the comparative rule, not the quantum, of the duty in either country is the only thing which concerns us, it is evident that our tobacco is much more favored by Great Britain than by France. Indeed the differences of duty operates as a positive bounty upon the tobacco of the United States.[37]

Regarding American navigation, comparison was more striking, Hamilton found. "Here too, we are more favored by Great Britain than other countries, while the existing regulations of France is in the degree the most exceptionable to be found in the code of any country. It amounts to a prohibition of carrying our own tobacco to France in our own ships." [38] The principle of such regulation would prostrate the navigation of the United States. In respect to the second most important staple of the United States, the regulations of Britain were more favorable than those of France. And, in addition, Britain was a far better customer than France.

The regulations of France on fish and fish oil, Hamilton found, were incomparably more favorable in their operation than those of Britain, "though there is no material difference in principle".[39] Britain excluded all but the finest oils and absolutely prohibited fish. French

[36]   *Ibid.*
[37]   *Ibid.*, 210-11.
[38]   *Ibid.*, 211.
[39]   *Ibid.*, 212.

distinctions of material aid to the United States were made in favor
of the whale fisheries, "but there is reason to apprehend, from the
means which have been successfully used to detach our fishermen,
and the vast encouragements which are given by the government,
that the whale fishery of France is establishing itself on the ruins of
that of the United States."[40] The natural advantages of the United
States in cod fishing made it difficult for them to be supplanted.
American ability to compete with French fisheries in French markets,
was attributable to the French incapacity to supply themselves, which
counteracted a system manifestly prohibitory in its principles. The
fact was, though, that the French dominions took from the United
States fisheries to the extent of $724,224 and those of Britain, only
$88,371.

French regulations had not made and did not make any distinction
as to wood, particularly lumber, in favor of the United States. Britain
put the citizens and ships of the United States upon the same footing
as her own colonies regarding the European market. Britain was a
better customer for this article than France.[41]

Rice stood upon a better footing in France than in Britain. In
France it was free. In Britain it was subject to a high duty. There
were no discriminations in either country in favor of the rice of the
United States. Hamilton noted, in passing, that as the article was not
produced in either country, and as United States rice was on the
same footing as that of other countries in British markets, the same
observations could be applied as were respecting tobacco, although
with less force, for tobacco had no competitors and rice did. The
British dominions took in value, $953,939 in 1790; the French
$322,926.[42]

Grain, namely wheat, rye, Indian corn, and oats, could be considered nearly in the same light as flour. All were free in the British
West Indies. Wheat and rye were prohibited in the French West
Indies and Indian corn and oats were admitted upon a one per cent
duty. "The result upon the whole is, that the English have been better
customers than the French."[43]

Pot and pearl ash stood in the past and in the present upon a better
footing by British regulations than by the French. In France the

---

40 *Ibid.*
41 *Ibid.*, 214.
42 *Ibid.*, 215.
43 *Ibid.*

United States and other countries competed on the same footing. In Britain, the pot and pearl ash of the United States was free, while those of other countries were subject to a 5 per cent duty. Britain took in 1790, $747,078 from the United States; France, $20,720.[44]

The eighth in value of American exports, indigo, stood upon a decidedly better footing in Britain. France was our competitor in the supply of her own market. The United States paid double the duty paid on her own by France. Britain admitted the article free of duty. Both countries excluded it from their West India markets.[45]

The regulations of both countries were equal in respect to live animals. France took $352,795 in 1790 and Britain took $62,415.[46] The regulations of Britain were more favorable in naval stores. Though the duties were higher in France, England laid higher duties on these articles when brought from other countries, than when brought from the United States. The difference was a bounty upon the productions of the United States. Britain took $96,832 of these articles, and France, $7,366.[47]

As to salted provisions, the regulations of France were evidently more favorable than those of Great Britain. Britain prohibited them.

The duties, however, are high, and even in respect to beef, are a serious incumbrance upon the sale with a living profit. In respect to pork, they amount essentially to a prohibition in France, which has great means of internal supply, and in the French West Indies the article is prohibited.[48]

No apparent differences existed in the regulations of the two countries respecting flaxseed, except that Britain was far the better customer. In iron, British regulations favored the United States — she admitted it free from duty. The regulations of France did favor the building of ships for sale over Britain, for United States built ships purchased by the French were naturalized in France. Such favor was now done away with. United States ships were entitled to be recorded in England and once recorded and owned by British subjects enjoyed the same privilege as British built ships in the trade between the United States and Britain.

A general distinction in favor of the United States runs through the regulations of Great Britain in this particular, that most articles of foreign

[44] *Ibid.*, 216.
[45] *Ibid.*
[46] *Ibid.*, 217.
[47] *Ibid.*
[48] *Ibid.*

countries brought in foreign ships, pay a higher duty than if brought in British ships; but not so of the same articles if brought in ships of the United States.[49]

In the West India trade of Britain, the United States had the advantage of their commodities being on the same footing as if brought from dominions of British North America. Salt, carried in United States ships, was favored in this trade.[50]

Hamilton's outline of the advantages American trade received from Britain above those of France are revealing. He showed that Britain was a much better customer than France for American goods and that Great Britain's commercial discriminations were more favorable to the United States than were those of France.

The advent of the Napoleonic Wars changed the position of the United States. Hamilton's economic structure would have been threatened in the event the United States was drawn into war. Our commerce would be annihilated to a great degree by a war, he warned. American agriculture would receive a deep wound with our commerce. The exports which animated it could not fail but be essentially diminished. Mechanics would share in the common calamity. The lively and profitable industry which was spreading a smile over American cities and towns would feel an instantaneous and rapid decay.

Nine tenths of our present revenues are derived from commercial duties. Their declension must of course keep pace with that of trade. A substitute cannot be found in other sources of taxation, without imposing heavy burdens on the people. To support public credit and carry on the war would suppose exactions really grievous. To abandon public credit would be to renounce an important means of carrying on the war; besides the sacrifice of the public creditors and the disgrace of national bankruptcy.[51]

However, he viewed the war as opening new avenues for neutral trade. As a neutral nation the United States now was in a stronger position to challenge British monopoly in the West Indies and increase her participation in the carrying trade. It was inevitable that a clash would occur between Britain's maritime policies and those of the upstart American nation and her French ally. Franco-American commercial relations had been satisfactorily established in 1778 and

[49] *Ibid.*, 218.
[50] *Ibid.*, 219.
[51] "Americanus", Feb. 8, 1794. Lodge, *Works*, IV, 87.

in theory were efficacious. Anglo-American commerce had never been officially regulated by treaty. The time was auspicious in 1794 for settling outstanding differences with Britain, and also for pursuing an even more advantageous commercial intercourse.

CHAPTER IV

TREATY VIOLATIONS?

Alexander Hamilton wrote in *The Federalist* of the humiliations under which the United States labored. We were, indeed, almost at the
last stage of national humiliation; scarcely anything remained which
could further wound America's pride or degrade our character as an
independent nation. "Are there engagements to the performance of
which we are held by every tie respectable among men?" he asked.
The treaty of 1783 was constantly and unblushingly violated. Did we
owe debts to foreigners and citizens which had been contracted in
time of great peril? These remained without being properly dis-
charged. Were valuable territories and posts of ours still in the possession of a foreign power which ought to have been surrendered
long since? "These are still retained, to the prejudice of our interests,
not less than to our rights", he answered. Could the United States
repel aggression? We had neither troops, treasury, or government.
Could we remonstrate with dignity? Before we could we must first
remove imputations on our own faith, he admonished. Did nature and
compact entitle us to a free participation in the navigation of the
Mississippi? No matter at present, the fact was that Spain excluded
us from it. Was public credit an indispensable resource in times of
public danger? The United States seemed to have abandoned its
cause as desperate and irretrievable. If commerce was of importance
to national wealth, ours was at the lowest point of declension. If
respectability in the eyes of foreign nations was a safeguard against
foreign encroachments, the imbecility of the United States government forbade them even to treat with us.[1]

The new Federal Constitution gave hope for erasing these humilia-
tions. Using the machinery of it and his own realistic perception,
Hamilton set out to revise the evaluation above. Due partially to
Hamilton's policies, violations of the 1783 treaty were discontinued;

[1] Lodge, *Federalist*, 84-5.

American debts were being satisfactorily paid; the western posts were returned to the United States under Jay's Treaty; the United States could boast of a stable treasury and government; American remonstrances were becoming meaningful; we had gained navigational rights on the Mississippi; public credit was well established; American commerce was thriving; and respect for America abroad was increasing, by the time he met his untimely death. Let us look now at the actual events as they verify Hamilton's revision of American humiliations.

Provisional articles of peace between Great Britain and the newly independent American states were signed in November 1782. Alexander Hamilton, in a letter to Washington, early forecast the problems which were proposed by the settlement. "Our affairs wear a most serious aspect as well foreign as domestic", he stated.[2] First appearance might lead to the conclusion that general peace was to be expected by the provisional articles, but strong reasons caused him to doubt such a conclusion. Obstacles could arise in different quarters, from Spain, Holland, and France, and more probably from the politics of Lord Shelburne. If peace did not take place, he feared that distrust would be sowed among the allies. He warned Washington that there were men in trust in America who hankered after a British connection, while the confidence others had in France savored of credulity. "The intrigues of the former and the incautiousness of the latter may be both, though in different degrees, injurious to the American course." [3]

Debate was lively and conflicting in Congress after news of the secret treaty arrived. Some members passionately demanded explanations for the actions of the commissioners in dealing separately with the enemy. Others defended their actions. It is interesting and important to study Hamilton's remarks on this issue, for they express the cogent reasoning which early assumed consequence in his career. His first recommendation was for "coolness and circumspection". Before proper judgment could be had on the conduct of the commissioners, it would be wise to examine the views of the British and French Courts. It was probable that French policy was motivated by matters of self interest. Additionally, however, the policy of Great

[2] Hamilton to Washington, March 17, 1783. Edmund Burnett (ed.), *Letters of Members of the Continental Congress* (Washington, Carnegie Institution, 1934), VII, 85.
[3] *Ibid.*

Britain should be remembered: ". . . survey the past cruelty & present duplicity of her councils, behold her watching every occasion & trying every project for dissolving the honorable ties which bind the U.S. to their Ally, & then say on which side our resentments & jealousies ought to lie."[4] While he had disapproved the instructions requiring our commissioners to submit to the advice of France, he now highly disapproved their conduct in not showing the preliminary articles to France before they signed them, which articles should not ever have been signed separately. "This conduct gave an advantage to the Enemy which they would not fail to improve for the purpose of inspiring France with indignation & distrust of the U.S."[5] The fear was not the formation of a coalition between France and Great Britain, but was in the destruction of mutual confidence between France and the United States. He recommended a middle course as best: commend the commissioners in general, for if they should be recalled or reprehended "they would be disgusted & head & foment parties in this Country"; and then communicate the separate article to France.[6]

The preliminary articles were ratified by the American Continental Congress in 1783; this step announced legal adherence to the stipulations therein contained, but there were, in fact, already decided doubts respecting the true construction of the provisional treaty. Hamilton, as a member of the Continental Congress from New York, was directly concerned with the perplexing questions which evolved.[7] One of the central questions concerned a matter of timing in Congressional discharge of the treaty. Hamilton contended that Congress was bound by the tenor of the provisional treaty to ratify it immediately, and to execute the several stipulations in it.[8] This stand was taken in dissent to a Congressional recommendation that a decision on ratification be postponed. However, the next day, Hamilton in a letter to Washington, explained some of the doubts which had arisen in Congress. The problem was this: the sixth article allowed for no future confiscations after the ratification of the treaty in the United States; the seventh article made the surrender of prisoners, evacua-

---

[4] Gaillard Hunt (ed.), *Journals of the Continental Congress, 1774-1789* (Washington, Government Printing Office, 1922), XXV, 932.

[5] *Ibid.*

[6] *Ibid.*, 933.

[7] Hamilton was chosen as a delegate to Congress in July 1782 and attended from November 1782 to July 1783, some eight months.

[8] Hunt, *op. cit.*, XXV, 960.

tion of the posts, cessation of hostilities, and so on, dependent on the ratification of the treaty in the United States. The doubt was "whether *the treaty* means the provisional treaty *already concluded* or the definitive treaty to be concluded".[9] While not fully clear in his own opinion, Hamilton made these suggestions, which reveal the sagacity of his thought. It was advisable not to communicate American doubts to the British, but to try to extract from them their sense of the matter. This could be done by asking when they would be willing to surrender the posts, he thought, while at the same time asking in what manner they could most conveniently receive the prisoners. Should the British postpone evacuating the posts to the definitive treaty, then the United States would be justified in doing the same with the prisoners. "I doubt the expedience of a total restoration of prisoners 'til they are willing to fix the epochs at which they will take leave of us." [10]

Even as Congress was debating, the several states were already showing signs of violating the treaty. Such behavior was a source of grief to Hamilton, who felt faithful observance of the treaty deeply interested the United States. An urgent statement of his views was made in a letter to Governor Clinton. Even though we could assume that the true policy of the British was to fulfill her engagements and cultivate the good-will of the United States, we should also remember that "passion makes us depart from the dictates of reason", and the United States had no way of knowing to whom the reins of government might fall in Britain. The United States was in no condition to force compliance with her claims, he felt; she ought to be cautious in her actions with so much at stake and "not openly provoke a breach of faith on the other side by setting the example".[11] "In the eye of a foreign nation, if our engagements are broken, it is of no moment whether it is for the want of good intention in the government, or for want of power to restrain its subjects." [12] He asked, would any foreign nation be willing to undertake anything with or for the United States, after it became known that the nature of her governments allowed no dependence to be placed on her engagements?

Some men said that the operation of the treaty was suspended until ratification of the definitive treaty. This was a plain subterfuge,

---

[9]   Hamilton to Washington, April 15, 1783. Burnett, *op. cit.* VII, 138.
[10] *Ibid.*, 139.
[11] Hamilton to Governor Clinton, June 1, 1783. Lodge, *Works*, IX, 344.
[12] *Ibid.*, 345.

Hamilton stated. The stipulations of the provisional or preliminary treaty were as binding from the beginning as the definitive treaty. The definitive treaty was merely a development, explanation and more precise description of what had been expressed in the provisional one. There were examples of years intervening between preliminary and definitive treaties. Would it be America's interest in such an event to countenance the position that nothing was binding till the definitive treaty? Hamilton thought not. Peace was necessary to Great Britain in his estimation, and she was not likely to renew the war. In fact, he thought "it also most probable her disposition to conciliate this country will outweigh the resentments which a breach of our engagements is calculated to inspire".[13] There was no sense in running this risk though, when the treaty had exceeded the hopes of the most sanguine and the United States was in no condition to make war again. Without recommencing hostilities, Britain could evade parts of the treaty by keeping possession of the posts, obstructing the free use of the fisheries, and failing to extend commercial concessions it was our interest to secure. There would be no foreign opposition to this action, and the United States was unable to oblige Britain to anything.

If the United States imagined that France would renew the war to force Britain to comply with our demands, it was random speculation. Hamilton wondered if the United States was prepared, simply for the gratification of her own resentments, to put the great national objects of the western frontier, the fur trade and the fisheries to the hazard. "Do we think national character so light a thing as to be willing to sacrifice the public faith to individual animosity?" [14]

The case could be fairly stated, Hamilton continued: two independent nations were at war, Great Britain and America. Great Britain possessed considerable posts and districts of territory belonging to America, and also the means of obstructing commercial advantages in which America was deeply interested. Usually the *uti possidetis* took place in peace treaties, but in this instance, Britain agreed to restore all our posts and territories in her possession, and readmit us to participation in the fisheries. And what equivalent might the United States give? Congress should recommend the restoration of property. This was the sole condition and the single equivalent for all the restitutions and concessions made by Great Britain.

[13] *Ibid.*
[14] *Ibid.*, 346.

Aware that some might misconstrue his real motives, Hamilton included in the letter a voucher for his interest:

Those who consult only their passions might choose to construe what I say as too favorable to a set of men who have been the enemies of the public liberty, but those for whose esteem I am most concerned will acquit me of any personal consideration, and will perceive that I only urge the cause of national honor, safety, and advantage. We have assumed an independent station; we ought to feel and to act in a manner consistent with the dignity of that station.[15]

In his "Letters from Phocion" Hamilton developed his concern for the consequences of the peace in a more comprehensive and revealing way. Men were urging the United States to become the scorn of nations by violating her solemn engagements, endeavoring to mould the treaty as it pleased them. In his opinion, the treaty spoke for itself. The fifth article was recommendatory, but the sixth was positive: no future confiscations were to be made, nor persecutions begun against any person or persons for or by reason of the part which they may have taken in the war; and no person, on that account, should suffer any future loss or damage in his person, liberty, or property. "Can we then do, by act of Legislature, what the treaty disables us from doing by due course of law?"[16]

Britain had made important concessions to the United States Hamilton again asserted. She was to surrender the immensely valuable posts on the frontier, and yield a tract of territory and one half the Great Lakes to the United States which would give us command of almost the whole fur trade. British claim to navigation of the Mississippi was renounced and our share in the fisheries was greater than it had been. Any man of sense would be ashamed to compare these concessions with what the United States was obliged to grant in return. There was a more forceful consideration which would certainly influence men who were superior to conscientious obligations. The United States was not in possession of the posts yet and could be excluded from the fisheries if the British were so disposed. To Hamilton, breach of treaty on the American part was a just ground for breaking it on their part. "The treaty must stand or fall together. The wilful breach of a single article annuls the whole. . . . One side cannot be bound, unless the obligation is reciprocal."[17] What if

---

[15] *Ibid.*, 349.
[16] "Letters from Phocion: To the Considerate Citizens of New York, on the Politics of the Times, in Consequence of the Peace", 1784. Lodge, *Works*, I, 237.
[17] *Ibid.*, 239-243.

Britain should refuse any further compliance with the treaty as a result of American breach of it, Hamilton wondered? What situation would we be in then? Could we renew the war to force compliance?

We know, and all the world knows, it is out of our power. Will those who have heretofore assisted us take our part? Their affairs require peace as well as ours; and they will not think themselves bound to undertake an unjust war, to regain to us rights which we have forfeited by a childish levity, and a wanton contempt of public faith.[18]

Moreover, Hamilton insisted, as evil attended American intemperance: the United States faced a loss of character in Europe.

Apparently Hamilton's statement that "the wilful breach of a single article annuls the whole" raised some objections among his readers. In the second "Letter to Phocion" he explained his conception of this principle. "The breach of one article annuls the whole, if the side injured by it chooses to take advantage of it to dissolve the treaty; but if its interest dictates a different conduct, it may waive the breach, and let the obligation of the treaty continue."[19] Since the power of determining whether the treaty had been broken resided in the body who made it, Congress had wisely proceeded on the presumption of its continuing in force, rather than declaring it void and resuming hostilities.

Britain made peace with America, Hamilton said, because the state of her affairs compelled her to do so. Britain labored under, and would for some time to come, "every species of embarrassment and disorder that a nation could experience", both internally and externally.[20] Some time would pass before she could be in condition to form enterprises against others.

When that period may arrive, our strength and resources will have greatly increased; the habits of men attached to her will have worn out: and it is visionary to suppose that she will then entertain a disposition to renew her attempts upon a country, increased in strength and resources, exerting its forces under an established Constitution, fortified by foreign alliances, which her acknowledged independence will at all times command; when she reflects that that country, in the tumult of a revolution, and in a state of comparative impotence baffled all her efforts in the zenith of her power.[21]

Special note should be paid to Hamilton's statements and reasoning

[18]   *Ibid.*, 243.
[19]   *Ibid.*, 264-65.
[20]   *Ibid.*, 281.
[21]   *Ibid.*, 282.

in his "Letters to Phocion", as they have relation to subsequent events, especially matters involving breach of treaty and obligation of contract. His pronouncement here will bear careful comparison with his stand later on the French Alliance in his principle of the means of extrication by virtue of national interest.

The Continental Congress after 1783 offered persistent objection to British violations of the treaty. The best that can be said for both sides, is that they were equally guilty. The Americans were more ready to admit this fact than were the British.[22] The British were indisposed to release the western posts, fully aware that the retention of them was a weapon of immeasurable manipulative importance. Her pretext for doing so was American violations of the treaty, while her real motives were to advance British control in Canada and the American hinterland. The British were conscious of the American commercial potential, and American interest in extending it was a useful tool. In this case, however, they were in a slightly less favorable position, since the American commercial trade benefited them also.

It was obvious to both sides that vital interests were at stake. John Adams succinctly expressed the British dilemma:

The British Ministry, therefore, have now before them a question as important to the British empire as any that ever was agitated in it; whether by evacuating the posts, and fulfilling the treaty of peace in other points, and by opening their ports in the West Indies and on the continent of America, as well as in Europe, to our ships and produce, upon equal and fair terms, they shall insure the impartiality and neutral-

---

[22] John Jay, in a letter to John Adams, then American minister to Great Britain, stated: "The result of my inquiries into the conduct of the States relative to the treaty, is, that there has not been a single day since it took effect, on which it has not been violated in America, by one or other of the States; and this observation is just, whether the treaty by supposed to have taken effect either at the date or exchange of the provisional articles, or on the day of the date of the definitive treaty, or of the ratification of it." Letter dated Nov. 1, 1786 in Henry Johnston, *The Correspondence and Public Papers of John Jay* (New York, G. P. Putnam's Sons, 1891), III, 214. Jay was also willing to admit American violations to the British. John Temple, British Consul General in the United States, in a dispatch to Lord Carmarthen, revealed an interesting conversation between himself and Jay in which Jay admitted as fact that his report to Congress was "a full acknowledgement that many of the most important Articles in Your Lordships Statement were just ... and consequently a violation of the subsisting Treaty. That His Majesty was every way justifiable in still holding the Western Posts until these States should Manifest a fair & honorable disposition to fulfill their part of the said Treaty." F.O. 4:4 [For year, 1786, no numbers recorded in Library of Congress.] Lib. Cong.

ity of America; or whether, by a contrary conduct, they shall force them into closer connections of alliance and commerce with France, Spain and Holland.[23]

The boundaries and politics of Europe were being reshaped; Britain was imminently concerned with the outcome, and the United States could well be a pawn in the machinations of the great powers unless she remained aloof and reserved.

The Continental Congress seemed to be as aware as Hamilton of the weak position of the United States.[24] However, they were much less urgent in remonstrating to the states at their infractions of the treaty than he, perceiving that their power was only recommendatory and if met with noncompliance would impair the little authority they did possess.[25]

Awareness of the impotency of the Confederation was climaxed by the Constitutional Convention. Hamilton and others had on numerous occasions decried the ineffective machinery of government under the Articles of Confederation, lamenting the lack of congressional control over matters domestic and foreign. Many of the protests to British evasions of the treaty met dilatory or inefficacious behavior largely due to the inability of the government to support its demands. British vascillation may have been partly necessitated by the insecurity of her international position.

The changes in governmental machinery under the new Constitution were momentous for the future of the United States. That such changes were needed cannot be doubted; the new government possessed the power necessary to build a nation. In 1783 Hamilton had prophetically written:

It now only remains to make solid establishments within to perpetuate the Union, to prevent our being a ball in the hands of European powers, bandied against each other at their pleasure; in fine to make our independence truly a blessing. This, it is to be lamented, will be an arduous work; for, to borrow a figure from mechanics, the centrifugal is

[23] Adams to Secretary Jay, October 17, 1785. John Adams, *The Works of John Adams* (Boston, Little, Brown & Co., 1854), VIII, 323.

[24] The Secretary for Foreign Affairs, Jay, reported on March 22, 1786, that the United States had threatened seeking French aid to demand British fulfillment of the treaty. On the 31st of March, Jay reported: "It would not be expedient to press that Answer [either war or disgrace in the event Britain refused to evacuate the posts] while the Intentions of the Court of France on the Subject remain doubtful." Adams should therefore be given instructions "to protract his Negociations" [sic.]. Hunt, *op. cit.*, XXX, 126-27, 147. See also *ibid.*, XXXII, 416.

[25] *Ibid.*, 243.

much stronger than the centripetal force in these States, — the seeds of disunion much more numerous than those of union.[26]

The need had become a reality. The United States was now provided with the means to bargain effectively on the international scene if she so chose, a fact which Hamilton had envisaged.

Upon assuming the presidency, Washington, in the hopes of resolving the differences between Britain and the United States, proposed sending an unofficial emissary to Great Britain to ascertain "the views of the British Court with respect to our Western Posts in their possession, and to a Commercial treaty".[27] Washington consulted Jay and Hamilton on the propriety of sending a private agent, and both thought it advisable. Hamilton recommended Gouverneur Morris for the mission.[28]

Morris was dispatched with instructions to the British Court. His correspondence of the ensuing conversations were submitted to Congress by Washington. The results were typical of the pattern observable from 1783:

... they [the British] declare without scruple they do not mean to fulfill what remains of the treaty of peace to be fulfilled on their part ... till performance on our part ... that, on the subject of a treaty of commerce, they avoided direct answers, so as to satisfy Mr. Morris they did not mean to enter one, unless it could be extended to a treaty of alliance offensive and defensive, or unless in the event of a rupture with Spain.[29]

Concurrent with the transpiring of these talks Beckwith had apparently been seeking an outlet for his proposal in the circles of American government. In Hamilton, who we will find encouraged seemingly intimate conversations, he found a listening ear. Whether other Americans listened to Beckwith is not known. Hamilton's official records indicate that he listened, answered and recorded, all with a degree of suspicion.[30]

---

[26]   Hamilton to Washington, March 24, 1783. Lodge, *Works*, IX, 327.
[27]   John Fitzpatrick (ed.), *The Diaries of George Washington* (Boston and New York, Houghton Mifflin Co., 1925), IV, 16.
[28]   *Ibid.*
[29]   American State Papers, *Foreign Relations* (Washington, Gales & Seaton, 1832), 1st Cong., 3rd sess., no. 50, Feb. 14, 1791, I, 121. Hereafter cited: *Foreign Relation Papers*.
[30]   Hamilton was not alone in his suspicions. Temple reported to the Duke of Leeds: "Lord Dorchester has had one of his aids de camp here, & at Philadelphia, for the year past! the stationing this Person about Congress hath indeed disgusted not a few, who heretofore leaned towards Great Britain. 'An Envoy, say they, from a Colony Governor, to a Sovereign Power, is a business heretofore

Beckwith approached Hamilton on the eighth of July speaking of the expected rupture between Spain and Britain and observing that it was one in which all commercial nations would favor the views of Britain. If a war should take place it could therefore be presumed, said Beckwith, that the United States would find it to her interest to take part with Britain. Beckwith produced a letter signed "Dorchester" containing ideas similar to those he expressed, in more guarded terms, and without allusion to instructions from the British Cabinet. Hamilton remarked that these seemed to be sentiments only of Lord Dorchester; Beckwith countered "that whatever reasons there might be for that course of proceeding in the present stage of the business, it was to be presumed that his lordship knew too well the consequences of such a step, to have taken it without a previous knowledge of the intentions of the cabinet".[31]

On the twenty-second of July, Beckwith and Hamilton had a second interview. (The reader should note Hamilton's conversational technique here and in the later Hammond exchanges.) Hamilton reminded Hammond that certainly his authority from Lord Dorchester was out of the question: ". . . I presume from his lordship's station and character, and the knowledge he appears to have of what is passing on the other side of the water, with regard to Mr. Morris, that the step he has taken through you is conformable to the views of your cabinet, and not without its sanction."[32] Beckwith was certainly sensible, Hamilton continued, that the business was presented in a shape which did not give it proper authenticity, and was wholly without formality. Beckwith was surely aware that there was a material difference between his situation and Morris' in London, for the credentials of Morris came from the proper source while Beckwith's were neither formal nor authoritative.[33]

Having noted this state of affairs and after assuring Beckwith that they would of course bear on what he had to say, Hamilton continued to speak. There was a sincere disposition in the government of the United States to view with candor and fairness all grounds of mis-

---

unheard of! he can be considered in no other light than as a petty Spy!'

What the purpose of Major Beckwith's being sent here, By What Authority he is here, — or, of what his Powers may be (if he has any in the diplomatic lines), I am totally ignorant!" May 23, 1791. F.O. 4:10, No. 70. Lib. Cong.

[31] Hamilton to Washington, Cabinet Paper, July 8, 1790. Lodge, *Works*, IV, 298.

[32] Hamilton to Washington, Cabinet Paper, July 22, 1790. Lodge, *Works*, IV, 299-300.

[33] *Ibid.*, 300.

understanding which existed "in reference to the execution of the late treaty of peace, and in laying the foundation of future good understanding, by establishing liberal terms of a commercial intercourse".[34] The project of an alliance opened a wide field, for the subject was susceptible of a vast variety of forms. Unless specific points were made clear, it was impossible to say what would be proper or what could be done, he told Beckwith. "If you are in condition to mention particulars, it may afford better ground of conversation." [35] Since Beckwith could say nothing more precise,[36] Hamilton said that if the subject should be presented in "authentic and proper shape", the United States would freely converse on it. "And you will naturally conclude that we shall be disposed to pursue whatever shall appear under all circumstances to be our interest, as far as may consist with our honor. At present I would not mean either to raise or repress expectations." [37]

Beckwith turned next to sound out Hamilton if there existed any connection between Spain and the United States and whether the Mississippi questions were settled. Hamilton declared without hesitation "That there was no particular connection between Spain and the United States, within my knowledge, and that it was a matter of public notoriety, that the questions alluded to were still unadjusted." [38] A postscript by Hamilton in his report to Washington of this conversation, noted that Jefferson was privy to the transaction. He explained his policy:

---

[34] *Ibid.*

[35] *Ibid.*

[36] Beckwith was in correspondence with Lord Grenville as is attested by an interesting report he made pointing out the great point of difference existing in the American government. "The great point of difference is one an English and a French connexion [sic]; the gentlemen at the head of the former, conceive the best interest of this country will be promoted by a solid and permanent friendship with Great Britain, and in this opinion he is supported by the most enlightened men in the legislature; this party think that the condition of the two countries is such as to render the formation of a commercial treaty very practicable and to the benefit of both nations and they are extremely desirous to promote it. . . ." Major Beckwith to Lord Grenville, March 11, 1791. F.O. 4:12. Lib. Cong.

[37] Lodge, *op. cit.*, 300-301.

[38] Morris in his London conversations was saying: "That the Spaniards being in fact apprehensive of danger from us, were disposed to make sacrifices for our friendship. That the navigation of the Mississippi, hitherto the bone of contention, was, I believed, given up by them already, or would be so; and as for their claims, they never could affect us, and therefore we did not care any thing about them." Morris to Washington, Sept. 18, 1790. *Foreign Relation Papers*, I, 127.

The views of this government were to discard suspicion that engagements with Spain, or intentions hostile to Great Britain, existed; to leave the ground in other respects vague and open, so as that in case of rupture between Great Britain and Spain, the United States ought to be in the best situation to turn it to account, in reference to the disputes between them and Great Britain on the one hand, and Spain on the other.[39]

This view was entirely in keeping with the policy of the government at that time.[40]

In late August Washington queried his heads of department on how to answer Lord Dorchester should he request permission to march troops through United States territory from Detroit to the Mississippi, in the event of war between Britain and Spain over Nootka Sound. He sketched the threat of having a formidable and enterprising people such as the British on both the front and rear flanks of the United States, seducing the western settlements, threatening the security of the Union and American commerce with the West Indies.[41]

Hamilton's reply came on the fifteenth of September. The first task of his reply was to assess the right to refuse or consent, "as shall be thought most for the interest of the United States".[42] Second, Hamilton set out to determine the consequences to be expected from refusal or consent, and lastly, the motives to the one or the other. If the question were to be decided upon principle only, without regard to opinions or precedents, refusal would follow without hesitation. Were the United States in condition to do it, she could adopt a rule never to grant passage for a voluntary expedition of one power against another, unless obliged by treaty to do so. However, the United States was in no condition to encounter hazards or establish rules repugnant to the accepted maxims or usages of nations. There existed, said Hamilton, in the practice of nations a vague pretension to a right of passage which afforded to the strong a pretext for claiming and exercising it when it suited their interests, making it dangerous for the weak to refuse, "and sometimes not less so to grant it".[43]

The following circumstances were against the propriety of a refusal,

[39] Lodge, op. cit., 302.
[40] As set down by Washington on Wednesday, July 14, 1790. Fitzpatrick, "Diaries", op. cit., 143.
[41] Fitzpatrick, "Writings", op. cit., XXXI, 102-03.
[42] Hamilton to Washington, Cabinet Paper, Sept. 15, 1790. Lodge, Works, IV, 314.
[43] Ibid., 318.

Hamilton reasoned: no connection existed between Spain and the United States which obliged the United States to grant passage; the passage asked would be down rivers and through uninhabited wilderness for the most part, causing no injury to citizen or settlement; and the number of troops would not be cause for serious alarm. A refusal, in light of these circumstances, would give the complexion of partiality to Spain and indisposition to Britain, "which may be represented as a deviation from the spirit of exact neutrality".[44] Only one reason supported the right of refusal: it would be safer to have two powerful but rival nations on our borders, than to have one pressing on both sides, "and in capacity, hereafter, by posts and settlements, to envelop our whole interior frontier".[45]

Hamilton now enunciated a recurring theme in much of his rationale. The United States should not forget that she had received essential succor from France in the Revolution and valuable countenance and some direct aid from Spain. Nor should we forget that France and Spain were intimate allies, and that a treaty connected France and the United States. It may be said, he noted, that obligations of gratitude required us to run some risk rather than concur in things prejudicial to either of them, even if it meant risk in favor of the nation against which they assisted us. Refinements of this kind, he warned, should be indulged in with caution. Gratitude was due only for a kindness or service done for the benefit of the party to whom it was performed. The following analysis would serve as a test of our true situation in regard to France and Spain, he thought.

Where the interest or benefit of the party performing is the predominant cause of it, however there may result a debt, in cases in which there is not an immediate adequate or reciprocal advantage, there is then not even a debt. If the motive of the act, instead of being the benefit of the party to whom it was done, should be a compound of the interest of the party doing it and of detriment to some other, of whom he is the enemy and the rival, there is still less room for so noble and refined a sentiment.[46]

The conclusion which could be drawn from what had been said, claimed Hamilton, was that there was a right either to refuse or consent as judged from the interest of the United States. The consequences of consent were threefold: as acquisition of the Floridas and Louisiana by the British would increase their means of annoying the United States by virtue of contiguity to a greater part of our territory

[44]   *Ibid.*, 319.
[45]   *Ibid.*
[46]   *Ibid.*, 321-22.

and increased facility to influence the Indians. And additional danger of the dismemberment of the western country would be possession of the key to the only outlet for the productions of that country. Finally, material injury would descend on the commerce of the Atlantic states in due time.

Hamilton continued, saying that a refusal ought to be accompanied by a resolution to support it, by the sword if necessary; that is, to oppose the passage if attempted. The consequences of refusal if not effectual "must be absolute disgrace or immediate war".[47] If we threw no impediment in Great Britain's way, good humor could beget greater moderation, and concessions could be made as the price of our future neutrality. Recognition of American right to navigate the Mississippi and possession of New Orleans would greatly mitigate apprehension from British conquest of the Floridas. Both the western posts and navigation of the Mississippi called for vigilant attention; they were both of importance to the United States. Securing the latter was essential to the unity of the empire. Should war take place, the United States could accomplish both by negotiation. Once the United States was committed on either side, the advantage of her position for negotiation would be gone. This country had to have an outlet for its commodities. "This was essential to its prosperity. . . . A war with Spain, when our affairs will have acquired greater consistency and order", said Hamilton, "will certainly be to be preferred to such an alternative. In an event of this sort, we should naturally seek aid from Great Britain. This would probably involve France on the opposite side, and effect a revolution in the state of our foreign politics."[48]

It was problematical that the possessions of Great Britain in Canada would ever be desirable to the United States, Hamilton thought. They were not essential to our prosperity. Excepting the question of the detention of the western posts, there was no necessary source of future collision with Britain. We therefore had a more urgent interest to differ with Spain than with Britain. This conclusion was made stronger if the United States admitted when it was able to make good her pretentions that the possession of territories at the mouth of the Mississippi were the key to her security. The same danger existed should the territories in question remain in the hands of Britain or Spain.

[47]   *Ibid.*, 329.
[48]   *Ibid.*, 336.

Now, it is manifest, that a government scarcely ever had stronger motives to avoid war, than that of the United States at the present juncture. They have much to dread from war; much to expect from peace; something to hope from negotiation in case of a rupture between Britain and Spain. ... These considerations are additional admonitions to avoid, as far as possible, any step that may embroil us with Great Britain. It seems evidently our true policy to cultivate neutrality. This, at least, is the ground on which we ought to stand, until we can see more of the scene, and can have secured the means of changing it with advantage.[49]

Hamilton saw the argument respecting consent or refusal as: if our refusal would prevent the acquisition of the Spanish territories bordering the United States, then we ought to refuse. But if there was considerable probability that our refusal would be ineffectual and war or disgrace ensue, and if war in our present condition was worse than the chances of the evils of that acquisition, then we ought not to refuse. This appeared to be the true conclusion to be drawn.

Lord Dorchester never requested passage. Hamilton's recommendations, although differing from those of his colleagues,[50] had laid down his views for a wise American foreign policy.

The matured reasoning Hamilton expressed regarding Great Britain and American foreign policy during the Nootka Sound controversy of 1791, had been suggested as early as 1783. In 1783, and in the succeeding years, Hamilton was concerned by violations of the peace treaty, fearing such violations would impair the benefits promised by the treaty. He regularly reminded Washington and his fellow citizens that to violate the treaty would only hurt America. Why should the United States offer Great Britain a chance or reason to withdraw the essentially beneficial allowances the treaty had included? Until the new nation had a satisfactory government, her future was certainly doubtful. Once the Federal Constitution was operational, the position of the country was strengthened, and Hamilton could with some assurance listen to and perhaps even bargain with Major Beckwith without a loss of dignity. In 1790 and 1791 the United States was little closer to assuming an offensive posture in Hamilton's reasoning. America's national interest was still intimately tied to Great Britain. The picture could change if and when official diplomatic relations were opened.

---

[49] *Ibid.*, 331-334.
[50] Jefferson advised that no answer should be given any request for passage, and should the British troops take silence for consent, their march could be pressed as a grievance. Adams argued for refusal.

CHAPTER V

DIPLOMAT WITHOUT PORTFOLIO

The British government officially opened diplomatic intercourse with the United States in 1791. George Hammond was sent as the King's Minister. Hamilton pridefully accounted for this turn of events. He gave the new constitution credit for raising the United States in the estimation of Europe. "According to the accounts received here, the change which has been wrought in the opinion of that part of the world respecting the United States is almost wonderful." [1] The British were even disposed now to enter into amicable and liberal arrangements with us, he noted.

Hammond's instructions were to negotiate those differences extant between the two countries respecting the peace treaty [2] and to explore the possibilities of a more liberal commercial agreement. Any such commercial treaty would have to be predicated upon complete reciprocity and the most favored nation. [3]

Phineas Bond, the British Consul at Philadelphia, had reported that those most concerned in the executive department of the American government viewed the benefits of British commerce and the western posts with a very jealous eye. [4] In March of 1791 he had communicated knowledge respecting United States proposals to regulate rigorously commerce with Great Britain despite the real impor-

---

[1] Hamilton to Benjamin Goodhue, June 30, 1791. Lodge, *Works*, IX, 483.
[2] "You are to consider this as the first and leading Object of your Mission." Lord Grenville to Hammond, Sept. 2, 1791. F.O. 4:11, No. 1. Published in: Bernard Mayo (ed.), *Instructions to the British Ministers to the United States 1791-1812* (Washington, Government Printing Office, 1941), 14. Hereafter cited: Mayo, *Instructions*.
[3] F.O. 4:11, No. 2. Mayo, Instructions, 17-19.
[4] Bond to the Duke of Leeds, Jan. 3, 1791. F.O. 4:9, No. 69. Published in: "Letters of Phineas Bond, British Consul at Philadelphia, to the Foreign Office of Great Britain, 1790-1794", *Annual Report of the American Historical Association, 1897* (Washington, Government Printing Office, 1898), 469-70.

tance of such trade to the revenue of the country.[5] Mindful of these reports, Hammond's instructions for regulating commercial intercourse were designed to raise American expectations, but only slightly. As to the posts, Hammond's instructions were more positive in their intent:

... these posts are of a great Service in securing the Fidelity and Attachment of the Indians, and as they offer to Great Britain the means of commanding the Navigation of the Great Lakes, and the communication of the said Lakes with the River St. Lawrence, they are certainly of great importance to the Security of Canada, and to the Interests of this Country, both in a commercial and political view. It is to be wished therefore that they should remain in His Majesty's possession, if the Conduct of the United States should continue to justify this measure on the part of Great Britain.[6]

Hamilton had suggested in his letter to Benjamin Goodhue that "if some liberal arrangement with Great Britain should ensue, it will have a prodigious effect upon the conduct of some other parts of Europe". This was followed in the next sentence by a more conservative statement to the effect that it would be wisest for the United States to depend as little as possible on the caprices of Europe, exerting ourselves, instead, "to the utmost to unfold and improve every domestic resource".[7] Hamilton's opportunity to promote such hope for making "some liberal arrangement with Great Britain" presented itself in a series of intimate conversations beginning in December 1791, between Hammond and himself. Hammond faithfully reported these to the home office, and in them can be seen the personal diplomatic strategy employed by Hamilton. These exchanges have been construed to indicate Hamilton's preference for Great Britain; to charge him with the attributes of a quisling nature. Rather, they show delicate manipulative techniques of suggestion,[8] the implanta-

---

[5] Bond to the Duke of Leeds, March 14, 1791. F.O. 4:9, No. 71. *Ibid.*, 476-80.
[6] Lord Hawkesbury's Draft of Instructions to Hammond, July 4, 1791. F.O. 4-10. Mayo, *Instructions*, 7.
[7] Lodge, *Works*, IX, 483.
[8] Hamilton suggested that Wolcott use this technique in 1796: "If the English had been wise, they would neither have harassed our trade themselves, nor suffered their trade with us to be harassed. They would see this as a happy moment for conciliating us by a clever little squadron in our ports and on the coast. A hint might perhaps do no harm." Hamilton to Wolcott, June 15, 1796. George Gibbs, *Memoirs of the Administrations of Washington and John Adams* (New York, William Van Norden, 1846), I, 360.
    Hamilton was still personally using the technique in 1797 when he expressed the opinion to Liston, the British minister, that Britain "ought carefully to avoid

tion of ideas, and a flexible mollifying method. Hamilton's technique was to imply much while saying little, to encourage trust in his every word, to indicate a possibility through half-statements. In other words, to cultivate a cozy, trustful atmosphere.

In December the two men had a long and confidential conversation in which Hammond's opinion of Hamilton's "just and liberal way of thinking was fully confirmed". Hammond expressed Britain's "sincere desire" to see peace between the Indians and the United States permanently re-established and suggested that if the United States should think it proper, the King's mediation through His government in Canada could be solicited. Hamilton replied that in the present war the United States had no motives for extending their territory, only the desire of binding down the Indians. If this could not be negotiated, the war would be prosecuted with vigor. Since the United States was, however, "sincerely solicitous to effect pacification, and if the voluntary interposition of the King's government in Canada could tend to accomplish it, such a measure would be received with the greatest gratitude." Hamilton hinted to Hammond, "with as much caution, as the danger of committing himself too far rendered necessary", that the present was an important crisis in the affairs of the United States upon which the future political connections and commercial arrangements with the nations of Europe depended. Hammond also gathered that France was holding out to the United States "some additional circumstances of advantage, which will have a tendency still farther to favor and promote the navigation of the United States". Hamilton informed him further that he was preparing a report on the actual state of navigation and commerce of the United States, in which he found that in balancing the systems of France and Britain, "the scale had hitherto decidedly preponderated in favor of the commercial encouragements afforded by Great Britain".[9]

The next month, January 1792, the two gentlemen discussed some of the questions likely to be subjects of negotiation between the two countries. Following some comments on the infractions specified by Jefferson, Hamilton "expressed conviction that the surrender of the posts was the only one which could produce any lengthy or difficult

---

urging the American Ministry to any stipulations, which might add strength to that imputation of partiality to Great Britain, which has of late been cast upon them by the Democratic Party. ..." Liston to Lord Grenville, Oct. 28, 1797. F.O. 5:33, No. 45. Lib. Cong.

[9] Hammond to Lord Grenville, Dec. 19, 1791. F.O. 4:11, No. 13. Lib. Cong.

investigation". (This had been one of Hamilton's points in his answer to Washington's queries during the Nootka Sound episode). Hamilton intimated that while the United States could not be induced to consent to a dereliction of any part of its territory acquired by treaty, it might "be possible to grant to his Majesty's subjects such privilege and immunities in the respective posts as would protect and secure them in the undisturbed prosecution of the Fur Trade". The matter of the negroes did not strike Hamilton as being an object of such importance as it did to other members of the government, Hammond found. Hamilton admitted to him the magnitude of the contraventions of the treaty by the United States; vindication for them could only be claimed on the "inefficiency of the former Congress to enforce respect to its own regulations". The chief ground of complaint for Britain was the subject of the British creditors, Hamilton felt, and this cause of complaint would be completely removed by the operation of the judiciary system. Respecting the commercial arrangements between the two countries, Hamilton "readily admitted the importance of the British commerce to the United States, and expressed his sanguine hopes that some system might be established mutually satisfactory to both Countries". He emphasized with force and emphasis the anxiety of the United States to obtain

a small participation in the carrying trade with the West Indies, and the expediency of granting it; subject nevertheless to such restrictions and regulation as Great Britain might require to limit the size and tonnage of the Vessels employed in the trade, and to prevent the ships of the United States from interfering in the exportation to Europe of the productions of the British West India Islands.

Hammond studiously avoided dropping any hint that Britain might even consent to a modification of her system.[10]

Hammond's suggestion for the tendering of the good offices of Britain in the American-Indian war, was officially recommended in March.[11] However, Hammond wrote in early February that he had

[10]   Hammond to Lord Grenville, Jan. 9, 1792. F.O. 4:14, No. 3. Lib. Cong.
[11]   The general grounds on which such an accommodation would be negotiated were: "the securing to the different Indian Nations, along the British and American Frontiers, their Lands and hunting Grounds, as an independent Country, with respect to which, both His Majesty and the United States shall withdraw all Claims or Possessions whatever, shall agree never to establish any Forts within the Boundaries to be expressed . . . and shall bind themselves to each other not to acquire . . . by purchase, or otherwise, from the Indians, any Lands or Settlements within the said Boundaries." Lord Grenville to Hammond, March 17, 1792. F.O. 115:1, No. 8. Mayo, *Instructions,* 25.

heard on pretty good authority that the government would not "accept or admit any intervention or mediation in the restoration of peace ... so long as the Posts shall remain in the possession of his Majesty's arms".[12] The instructions and report were traveling in cross-packets.

Complying with a request to sound Hamilton out on the Short-Carmichael negotiations with Spain, Hammond inquired if the object of the commission was to negotiate a treaty relative to the navigation of the Mississippi. Hamilton answered in the affirmative, adding that this and other points of a like nature had been subjects of frequent disagreement and discussion between the two governments. Hammond reminded Hamilton of British treaty rights in this regard and trusted that the United States would not make any agreement which might militate against these rights and interest. "Mr. Hamilton assured me that this government was far from entertaining any such intention, as neither their interest nor inclination would prompt them to adopt any measures which might affect the rights, to which I had alluded." Hammond was inclined to believe Hamilton.

For from combining it with some accidental observations, that he formerly threw out on the subject of the Mississippi in one of our earliest conversations, I am led to infer that this government esteem the participation of Great Britain in the navigation of that river, as an object of benefit, rather, than disadvantage. . . .

In another part of the conversation, when Hammond affected to speak lightly of the general politics of the Court of Spain, Hamilton said, "with some degree of quickness, that 'it is indeed very singular that they have never proposed anything which has not been clogged by some strange absurd impediment or another' ".[13]

Hammond broached the subject of British mediation and the idea of an independent Indian nation to Hamilton in June. In his earliest conversations with that gentleman, he had met resistance to such insinuation, Hammond stated.[14] On this occasion Hamilton did not equivocate in his reply but was explicit. He

did not attempt to enter into any discussion of the arguments ... but replied briefly and coldly, that he wished me to understand that any plan, which comprehended anything like a cession of territory, or right,

[12] Hammond to Lord Grenville, Feb. 2, 1792. F.O. 4:14, No. 8. Lib. Cong.
[13] Hammond to Lord Grenville, April 5, 1792. F.O. 4:14, No. 15. Lib. Cong.
[14] Hamilton had been interested in such a possibility, but with reservations. See *ante*, 93.

or the allowance of any other power to interfere in the disputes with the Indians, would be considered by this government as absolutely impracticable and inadmissible.[15]

Hammond decided that it would not be wise to make a formal offer of mediation; not only would it "be instantly rejected, but would also excite considerable jealousy of the real views and wishes of his Majesty's government".[16]

Hammond's formal exchanges were transacted with Jefferson, the Secretary of State. These were highly frustrating to both individuals and their governments. Upon the occasion of receiving an answer from Jefferson to one of his statements, Hammond was considerably surprised. He therefore waited upon Hamilton to voice his opinion of this "extraordinary performance". Hamilton treated Hammond with "the strictest confidence and candour", and lamented the intemperate behavior of his colleague. He assured Hammond that Jefferson's letter did not meet his approbation nor did it contain a faithful exposition of the sentiments of the United States government. He also added the information that Washington had not had an opportunity to read it.[17]

Casual conversations were had with Jefferson and Knox, as well as with the Secretary of the Treasury, on the feasibility of an independent Indian nation. The sentiments of the three coincided. Hammond reported that they "asserted that any plan of conciliation with Indians, which involved a cession of territory to any considerable extent, was perfectly incompatible with present views of this government, and would be far from meeting the approbation of the country". All three gentlemen uniformly expressed readiness to consent to any conditions respecting the western posts, "which Great Britain may deem essential to the security of any interests commercial or political". They were willing to enter any precise stipulations to limit the number of troops stationed at the forts, the number to be mutually maintained on the respective shores, and the naval force on the Lakes. They would further consent to any measure the government of Canada thought necessary to the security and protection of the persons and property engaged in the fur trade and commerce on the Lakes. Hammond reported these to be the general terms to which the United States "would accede with alacrity in order to effect a

15   Hammond to Lord Grenville, June 8, 1792. F.O. 4:15, No. 23. Lib. Cong.
16   Hammond to Lord Grenville, June 13, 1792. F.O. 4:15, No. 25. Lib. Cong.
17   Hammond to Lord Grenville, June 8, 1792. F.O. 4:15, No. 22. Lib. Cong.

cession of the posts". Hamilton added to this list. He said that his government would "consent to grant to the subjects of the crown a free intercourse of commerce with the Indians dwelling within the American territory, provided that a similar intercourse with the Indians residing in the territory of Canada should be allowed to the citizens of the United States".[18]

American negotiations with Spain over the Mississippi continued and Hammond maintained his vigil on their progress. He incidentally mentioned some circumstances relative to the Mississippi and then inquired as to the actual state of the negotiations. Hamilton informed him that they were pretty well advanced, but the Spanish government refused any cession of a seaport communication with the Mississippi. Since this was absolutely necessary, and he presumed it could not be effected by negotiation, "The necessity of obtaining it by any means must at some period ultimately lead to a rupture between" the United States and Spain. Hammond reaffirmed Britain's interests and rights, and hoped that "whenever the subject came into discussion", Britain would find the United States "inclined to such a regulation of the boundaries as would afford to his Majesty's subjects an effectual communication with the Mississippi". Hamilton replied that "it would well deserve the attention of the United States to consent to as liberal a measure of accommodation in that respect as would not be detrimental to their own interests". Even though this information varied somewhat from other reports, Hammond was inclined to believe Hamilton: "As in my communications with him I have never yet at any time had reason to suspect him of artifice or imposition." [19]

Late in 1792 the Indians sent a formal message to Governor Simcoe in Canada soliciting the British King's good offices. This was, of course, the next best thing to an appeal by the United States government for Britain. Hammond informed Hamilton of this event. Hamilton thanked him, but

expressed his persuasion that this government would not deem it expedient to accede to the Indian proposition of mediation — since he conceived that such a proceeding would diminish the importance of the United States in the estimation of the Indians, and might eventually lead to a disagreeable discussion with Great Britain. . . .[20]

[18] Hammond to Lord Grenville, July 3, 1792. F.O. 4:16, No. 26. Lib. Cong.
[19] Hammond to Lord Grenville, July 3, 1792. F.O. 4:16, No. 27. Lib. Cong.
[20] Hammond to Lord Grenville, Dec. 4, 1792. F.O. 4:16, No. 42. Lib. Cong.

The scene of war opened the year 1793. Great Britain and France were at war, and the role the United States would assume was of immediate concern to both adversaries. Hammond was warned in reference to the defensive treaty between the United States and France:

Nor will it escape you that every consideration of the Interests of the United States, must lead them to avoid an interference which is not called for by the terms of the subsisting Treaty, and which must necessarily involve them in the most serious misunderstanding with this Country.[21]

The British were not sure how the United States would view its treaty obligations with France as it bound her to come to the aid of France in the event of a defensive war. If the United States remained neutral, Britain's interests would be better served.

Hamilton's decisions regarding the best policy for the United States to follow, were made final by March. He assured Hammond that he would

exert his influence to defeat the success of any proposition on the part of France, which tempting as it might appear, might ultimately render it necessary for this government to depart from the observance of as strict a neutrality as is compatible with its present engagements, and which is so essential to its real interests.

Hammond felt secure in accepting Hamilton's statement, for he believed "that any event which might endanger the external tranquillity [sic] of the United States would be as fatal to the system he has formed for the benefit of his country, as to his present personal reputation and to his future projects of ambition".[22]

Washington posed a group of thirteen questions in April covering the whole range of American relations with the war, to his department heads.[23] Almost immediately the cabinet unanimously agreed to issue a proclamation forbidding American citizens to participate in the hostilities on the seas, and warning them against carrying any

[21] Lord Grenville to Hammond, Feb. 8, 1793. F.O. 115:2, No. 3. Mayo, *Instructions*, 35.
[22] Hammond to Lord Grenville, March 7, 1793. F.O. 5:1, No. 6. Lib. Cong.
[23] Jefferson claimed in his *Anas* that these questions were really Hamilton's and cites Randolph as his authority. Andrew Lipscomb (ed.), *The Writings of Thomas Jefferson* (Washington, The Thomas Jefferson Memorial Association, 1905), I, 267-68.

For the questions see: Washington to Hamilton, Cabinet Paper, April 18, 1793. Lodge, *Works*, IV, 366-68.

contraband articles to the belligerent powers. Thereupon, Washington issued a Proclamation of Neutrality.[24]

The answers which Hamilton gave to Washington's questions were detailed and complete; his sagacity and persuasive genius were lucidly displayed. His conclusion succinctly stated was: the interests of the United States compelled her to remain neutral.[25] If the United States plunged into the contest with France, the contest she found herself in would possibly be more unequal than the one France found herself engaged in. British and Spanish possessions were on both our flanks; Indian tribes under the influence of Britain and Spain were along our whole interior frontier; and we had an unprotected extended seacoast with no fortifications whatever and only a four million population, which would have the maritime force of all Europe against us. A more unequal contest could not be imagined, said Hamilton. The United States was dissuaded from such a contest by the most cogent motives of self-preservation, no less than of interest.[26]

Although the United States pursued a neutral policy, her difficulties with Great Britain continued. The Treaty of 1783 was still in limbo and United States shipping was suffering under the British definition of neutral trade. War was fast becoming the only solution to their differences. By 1794 it was an assumed eventuality. Hamilton was as provoked as were his countrymen, yet his voice sounded out for moderation. War was costly both financially and politically, and especially for a new nation whose international reputation was being established and still in doubt. To suffer loss of face and pride, to be disgraced in the minds of the world, this could not be sanctioned — passions should not replace reason.

Early in 1794 Hamilton published an interpretation of the effects war between Britain and the United States would have. War between the two could not fail but be distressing to Britain, and it would be weak to calculate on any decisive influence accruing from the circumstances. Britain's credit and commerce were still strong and it was not likely that war would "arrest her career, or overrule those paramount considerations which brought her into her present situa-

[24] *Foreign Relation Papers*, I, 140.
[25] Hamilton assiduously protected American neutrality, fearing the consequences of breaking it would involve the United States in war. For examples see: Lodge, *Works*, IV, 408-17.
[26] "Pacificus", No. III, July 6, 1793. Lodge, *Works*, IV, 458.

tion".[27] The United States must remember that Britain maintained herself for seven years under a privation of American commerce, while united for certain periods against France, Spain and Holland: "... we cannot reasonably doubt that she would be able, notwithstanding a similar privation, to continue a war...."[28] The United States was enjoying at that time

an unexampled state of prosperity. That war would interrupt it need not be affirmed. We should then by war lose the advantage of that astonishing progress in strength, wealth, and improvement, which we are now making, and which, if continued for a few years, will place our national rights and interests upon immovable foundations.... If, while Europe is exhausting herself in a destructive war, this country can maintain peace, the issue will open to us a wide field of advantages, which even imagination can with difficulty compass.[29]

Moreover, if we considered the naval superiority of the enemies of France, there could be no doubt that American commerce would be annihilated to a very great degree by war. American agriculture would receive a deep wound and American mechanics would share in the common calamity. "Nine tenths of our present revenues are derived from commercial duties. ... A substitute cannot be found in other sources of taxation, without imposing heavy burthens on the people."[30]

Hamilton continued, suggesting an Indian war excited by the united influence of Britain and Spain, would spread desolation throughout the American frontier.

The first collision between Britain and Spain would indubitably have one of two effects, either a temporary reunion of the whole country under Great Britain, or a dismission of the yoke of both.... If the first step was a reunion under Great Britain, the second, and one not long deferred, would be a rejection of her authority.[31]

Such a project would be absurd. The enterprise to Great Britain would threaten serious consequences: "... she would run by it greater risks of bankruptcy and revolution than we of subjugation ... she would make war upon her own commerce and credit."[32] Powerful motives of self-interest would advocate the American cause to Britain

---

[27] "Americanus", Feb. 1 and 8, 1794. Lodge, *Works*, V, 85.
[28] *Ibid.*
[29] *Ibid.*, 86.
[30] *Ibid.*, 87.
[31] *Ibid.*, 92.
[32] *Ibid.*, 93.

and the conduct of the United States would "entitle us to the reverse of unfriendly or hostile dispositions".[33] In effect, Hamilton was saying, that the interests of the two countries recommended the adjustment of their differences, and Britain would be inclined to negotiate.

In March Hamilton proffered to Washington the seriousness of the situation. The critical times demanded vigorous though prudent measures. "We ought to be in a respectable military posture because war may come upon us, whether we choose it or not; and because, to be in a condition to defend ourselves, and annoy any who may attack us, will be the best method of securing our peace."[34] The principal ports should be fortified, 20,000 auxiliary troops raised, and the Legislature should vest the President with the power to lay an embargo and arrest the exportation of commodities.

The following month brought forth Hamilton's personal recommendations for a course of action. The suggestions had not been solicited by Washington, but were voluntarily submitted by Hamilton on the excuse that "In such a crisis it is the duty of every man, according to his situation, to contribute all in his power towards preventing evil and producing good."[35] Hamilton first outlined the views of three parties existing in their councils: one, decided on preserving peace; another, decided for war; and a third, not absolutely desirous of war, but interested in continuing to excite the ill-humor existing between the United States and Britain. While it might be difficult to admit that parties of the last two descriptions existed, an explanation could be found in the course of human passions.

Wars oftener proceed from angry and perverse passions, than from cool calculations of interest. This position is admitted without difficulty when we are judging of the hostile appearances in the measures of Great Britain toward this country. What reason can there be why it should not be as good a test of similar appearances on our part? As men it is equally applicable to us, — and the symptoms are strong of our being readily enough worked up into a degree of rage and frenzy, which goes very far toward silencing the voice of reason and interest.[36]

The members of those parties whose measures had a war aspect, Hamilton felt, were influenced by some of the strongest passions

---

[33] *Ibid.*, 94.
[34] Hamilton to Washington, March 8, 1794. Lodge, *Works*, X, 63.
[35] Hamilton to Washington, Cabinet Paper, April 14, 1794. Lodge, *Works*, V, 97.
[36] *Ibid.*, 99-100.

actuating human conduct. They were united by an implacable hatred of Britain and warm attention to France. They sought revenge upon a detested enemy in hostility with Britain. They anticipated a great political good, a more complete and permanent alienation from Britain and a closer approximation to France. What of the general public? Here too could be found a considerable diversity of opinion, but on the whole the country was opposed to war. In light of the state of the public mind, if measures should be adopted,

which in the event should appear to have been obstacles to a peaceable adjustment of our differences with Great Britain, there would be, under the pressure of the evils produced by them, a deep and extensive dissatisfaction with the conduct of the government — a loss of confidence in it, and an impatience under the measures which war would render unavoidable. . . . war . . . may prove to be the threshold of disorganization and anarchy.[37]

Hamilton insisted that the necessity of war was not yet apparent: "There is room to suppose that the moment is peculiarly favorable" for negotiation.[38] While all ostensibly agreed that one more experiment of negotiation ought to precede actual war, there was a difference in their approach.

The sincere friends of peace and accommodation are for leaving things in a state which will enable Great Britain, without abandoning self-respect, to do us the justice we seek. The others are for placing things upon a footing which would involve the disgrace or disrepute of having receded through intimidation.[39]

The last scheme could lead only to war. To entertain such a position, that Britain would submit to our demands when fortified by alliances with the greatest part of Europe, was folly. To do so, Britain would have to renounce her pride and dignity without losing her consequence and weight in the scale of nations. It was morally certain she would not and any proper estimation of human passions would recognize the fact that Britain would be less disposed to receive the law from the United States than from any other nation. We were yet a new nation and only recently one of her dependencies.[40]

If a nation meant to negotiate before it went to war, Hamilton insisted, the usual course was to prepare for war, and proceed to negotiation while avoiding reprisals. In preparation for war there

[37] *Ibid.,* 102-103.
[38] *Ibid.,* 104.
[39] *Ibid.,* 105.
[40] *Ibid.*

was nothing offensive. But the propositions of the House of Representatives for the sequestration of British debts and the cutting off
of all intercourse with Britain were provocatives to a declaration of
war by Great Britain. The principle of the sequestration of debts
was coercive, "a principle directly opposite to that of negotiation,
which supposes an appeal to the reason and justice of the party".[41]
Aside from the tendency of these measures to produce war, Hamilton
felt, they could not help but have "a malignant influence upon our
public and mercantile credit".[42] To distress Britain seriously, the
United States would need to prohibit all her commodities. This would
deprive the United States of a supply for which no substitute could
be found elsewhere, a supply necessary to us in peace, and more
necessary to us if we were to go to war. Our revenue would receive
a serious blow:

It will give so great an interruption to commerce as may very possibly
interfere with the payment of the duties which have heretofore accrued,
and bring the Treasury to an absolute stoppage of payments — an event
which would cut up credit by the roots. The consequences of so great
and so sudden a disturbance of our trade, which must affect our exports
as well as our imports, cannot be calculated.[43]

Hamilton reminded Washington that: " 'Tis as great an error for a
nation to overrate us as to underrate itself. 'Tis our error to overrate
ourselves and underrate Great Britain; we forget how little we can
annoy, how much we may be annoyed." [44] The United States and the
President had to decide, in Hamilton's opinion, whether the plan
ought to be preparation for war and unincumbered negotiation,
or immediate coercive measures and a demand for redress. If the
former was chosen, he would suggest this course: nomination of a
person possessing the confidence of those seeking peace as Envoy
Extraordinary to Britain to negotiate the differences, and vigorous
and effectual preparations for war at home.

We have seen that with the opening of Anglo-American ministerial
channels in 1791, Hamilton's opportunities increased to pursue his

---

[41] *Ibid.*, 107.
[42] *Ibid.*, 108.
[43] Hamilton to Washington, Cabinet Paper, April 14, 1794. Lodge, *Works*, V,
109. The British were also aware of the importance of their trade to the United
States. Great Britain was "the most important consumer of the productions of
the Country [America] and the principal source of its revenue". Lord Grenville
to Phineas Bond, Oct. 10, 1795. F.O. 115:4, No. 1. Mayo, *Instructions*, 96.
[44] *Ibid.*, 110.

hopes for amicable settlement of outstanding difficulties between the two countries. His conversations with Hammond indicate the calculated activity of his interest. Hamilton rarely allowed the content of their conversation to stray from the ultimate aim of his goal. Nor would Hamilton allow war between Britain and France to interrupt the course of American neutrality. The neutral path in Hamilton's view was the only one which could bring the United States through the weaker periods of her growth to prosperous maturity. Furthermore, neutrality would assure Great Britain of American intentions to seek nonalignment with any foreign power. By pursuing a neutral policy the United States placed no new obstructions in the way of the existing Anglo-American quandary. An envoy extraordinary to Great Britain, of Hamilton's own choosing, would be one further step towards settlement.

CHAPTER VI

JAY'S TREATY

Hamilton's recommendations were well taken by Washington, and at his suggestion, Washington nominated John Jay as Envoy Extraordinary to Great Britain the next month. Hamilton was surely as provoked as were his fellow countrymen by the British, and though he recommended conciliation for the government, his own feelings erupted to the surface on occasion. They, interestingly enough, were vented on Hammond. Hammond took the occasion of a conversation with Hamilton, to communicate to him "confidentially and informally the very conciliatory explanations ... of the instructions of the 6th of November and of the modifications of them on the 8th of January. . . ." He was much surprised when Hamilton did not receive these explanations with cordiality, "but entered into a pretty copious recital of the injuries which the commerce of this country had suffered from British criuzers [sic], and into a defense of the consequent claim which the American citizens had on their government to vindicate their rights." Later in the conversation, Hammond reported that Hamilton "interrupted him in some degree of heat and remarked that however the government people of Great Britain might be united against France, he doubted not that where the wrongs which the American commerce had suffered were known in Great Britain, a very powerful party might be raised in that nation in favor of this country". When Hammond rechecked Hamilton's demand for indemnification for all American vessels captured by British cruisers as a condition indispensable to amicable adjustment, Hamilton reassured him that his meaning had not altered. Hammond reported that the United States was in popular ferment against Britain and now even Hamilton's feelings, which had been hitherto "uniformly the most moderate of the American Ministers", were much excited.[1]

Hamilton aided considerably in constructing Jay's instructions for

[1] Hammond to Lord Grenville, April 17, 1794. F.O. 5:14, No. 15. Lib. Cong.

negotiation. Washington respected the Secretary of the Treasury's opinions as they were always cogitable and rational. He asked Hamilton to make suggestions for points to be considered in Jay's instructions, and Hamilton's memorandum came to make up the central points of those instructions.² Jay's final instructions took their tenor from Hamilton's recommendations and alternatives, so that Jay's powers became virtually discretionary.³ Hamilton's letter to Jay ac-

² Hamilton to Washington, Cabinet Paper, April 23, 1794. Lodge, *Works*, V, 115-19.
³ "Instructions to Jay as Envoy Extraordinary" are found in Henry P. Johnston (ed.), *The Correspondence and Public Papers of John Jay* (New York, G. P. Putnam's Sons, 1891), IV, 11-20.
Hamilton's recommendations to Washington are dated April 23, 1794 and found in: Lodge, *Works*, V, 115-19.
A good deal of difficulty arose over the ambiguity of these instructions when the House of Representatives requested them during the appropriations sessions of 1796. The success of the treaty was threatened, but because the negotiation papers were in such a state, the call to see them was denied. Hamilton wrote: "I am not, however, without fear that there are things in the *instructions* to Mr. Jay — which good policy, considering the matter *externally* as well as *internally*, would render it inexpedient to communicate." Hamilton to Washington, March 24, 1796. Lodge, *Works*, X, 151. Washington was of like mind: "An attentive examination however of the Papers and the subject, soon convinced me that to furnish *all* the Papers would be highly improper, and that a *partial* delivery of them would leave the door open for as much calumny as the entire refusal. . . ." Washington to Hamilton, Private, March 31, 1796. Fitzpatrick, *Writings*, XXXV, 7.
Hamilton enumerated the reasons for not making the papers public:
"The truth, unfortunately, is that it is in general a crude mass, which will do no credit to the administration. This was my impression of it at the time, but the delicacy of attempting too much reformation in the work of another head of department, the hurry of the moment, and a great confidence in the person to be sent, prevented my attempting that reformation.
There are several particular points in it which would have a very ill effect to be published.
I. — There is a part which seems to admit the idea that an adjustment might be made respecting the spoliations which should leave that matter finally to the *ordinary course* of the British courts. This is obscurely and ambiguously expressed, but the least color for such a construction would give occasion for infinite clamor.
II. — The negotiator is expressly instructed to accede to the *entire abolition of alienism* as to inheritances of land. You have seen what clamor has been made about the modification of this idea in the treaty, and can thence judge what a load would fall on this part of the instructions.
III. — He is instructed to enter into an article against the employment of privateers in war. This is manifestly against the policy of a country which has no *navy* in a treaty with a country which has a large navy. For it is chiefly by privateers that we could annoy the trade of Great Britain. Some would consider this as a philosophic whim; others as an intentional sacrifice of the interests of this country to Great Britain.

companying the instructions revealed the latitude he conceived for the negotiation, and since the two men were very close in friendship and sympathies, Hamilton was able to spell out for Jay the prices to be paid for the items bought. The *"mere appearance* of indemnification" for depredations on American ships would not be satisfactory, but a *"substantial* indemnification", not complete or absolute indemnification, would be admissible.⁴ Even more,

If you [Jay] can effect solid arrangements with regard to the points unexecuted of the treaty of peace, the question of indemnification may be managed with less rigor, and may be still more laxly dealt with, if a truly beneficial treaty of commerce, embracing privileges in the West India Islands, can be established. It will be worth the while of the government of this country, in such case, to satisfy, itself, its own citizens who have suffered.⁵

In a commercial sense, the United States was more important to Britain than any other country, Hamilton contended. The articles she took from us were precious to her. They were important, perhaps even essential to the subsistence of her island, and not unimportant to her own subsistence occasionally. American articles were always very important to her manufactures and of real consequence to her revenue. The United States was the unrivalled consumer of British exports. We consumed a million and a half sterling more in value than any other foreign nation. Furthermore, consumption in the United States was increasing and for a long series of years would continue to increase rapidly. And, though our manufactures were no doubt progressive, our population and means were progressing so much faster that our demand for manufactured goods far exceeded

---

IV. — There are several parts which hold up the disreputable and disorganizing idea of not being able to *restrain our own citizens*.

V. — There are parts the publication of which, though proper to our own agent, would be a violation of decorum towards Great Britain, after an amicable termination of the affair, and offensive because contrary to the rules of friendly and respectful procedure.

VI. — The instructions have too little point (in the spirit of the framer, who was in the habit of saying much and saying little), and would be censured as altogether deficient in firmness and spirit."

"On the whole, I have no doubt that the publication of these instructions would do harm to the Executive, and to the character and interest of the government."

Hamilton to Washington, March 28, 1796. Lodge, *Works*, X, 152-54.

⁴ Hamilton to Jay, Cabinet Paper, May 6, 1794. Lodge, *Works*, V, 124.

⁵ *Ibid.*, 124-25. Hamilton had told Hammond that indemnifications were absolutely necessary. See *ante*, 113-14.

our own faculty to manufacture. Hamilton thought this would be the case for an incalculable period of time.[6]

With regard to the West Indies, Hamilton apprised Jay of an existing act of Parliament which allowed foreign European vessels, not exceeding seventy tons, to carry particular enumerated articles to and from certain British ports in the islands.

This consequently puts an end to the question of precedent, which is so strongly urged against a departure from the British navigation act in our favor, since it gives the precedent of such a departure in favor of others, and to our *exclusion* – a circumstance worthy of particular notice.[7]

A treaty of commerce on the footing of the status quo, for a short period, was admissible *only* in the event the unexecuted points of the peace treaty were satisfactorily settled. And, though such a treaty ought not to be *concluded* without reference to the United States for further instruction, Hamilton suggested that: "It is desirable, however, to push the British ministry in this respect to a result, that the extent of their views may be ascertained." [8]

The topic which completed Hamilton's "few loose observations" to Jay concerned navigation of the Mississippi, which was to the United States "an object of immense consequence".[9] If the United States could procure and secure the enjoyment of it to her Western country, it would become a "strong link of union between that country and the Atlantic States".[10] Anything that could be done with Britain to increase the chances of the United States for a more speedy enjoyment of this right, would be, in Hamilton's judgment, a valuable ingredient in any arrangement Jay could make. British interest was not wanting, so the United States might promise her participation in the navigation and a treaty of commerce into that large field of commercial adventures, as an inducement. "May it not be possible to obtain a guaranty of our right in this particular from Great Britain, on the condition of mutual enjoyment and a trade on the same terms as to our Atlantic ports?" [11] The subject was delicate and not fully matured in his mind, Hamilton admitted; particularly delicate because not unpromising negotiations were pending with Spain.

Hamilton had preferred his observations with a cautionary state-

[6] Hamilton to Jay, Cabinet Paper, May 6, 1794. Lodge, *Works*, V, 125-26.
[7] *Ibid.*, 127.
[8] *Ibid.*
[9] *Ibid.*
[10] *Ibid.*, 128.
[11] *Ibid.*

ment which would absolve him or the government from charges of misconstruing American interests. The statement seems to indicate a respect for popular political obsequiousness.

We are both impressed equally strongly with the great importance of a right adjustment of all matters of past controversy and future good understanding with Great Britain. Yet, important as this object is, it will be better to do nothing, than to do anything that will not stand the test of the severest scrutiny — and especially, which may be construed into the relinquishment of a substantial right or interest.[12]

Jay's appointment was fortunate for the successful execution of Hamilton's instructions. Both men were in accord with the purpose of the mission and they shared a sympathetic understanding of its importance. Jay's correspondence with Hamilton during the negotiations reveals this consanguinity. In mid-July 1794 Jay wrote "My Dear Sir" that nothing decisive could be reported. "Appearances continue to be singularly favourable, but appearances merit only a certain degree of circumspect reliance." [13] He said he had dined with Lord Grenville shortly after his arrival and would be dining with the Lord Chancellor and Pitt soon.

I mention these facts to explain what I mean by favourable appearances. I think it best that they should remain unmentioned for the present, and they make no part of my communications to Mr. Randolph, or others. This is not the season for such communications; they may be misinterpreted, though not by you.

I fear the posts may labour, but they must not be left. We must not make a delusive settlement; that would disunite our people, and leave the seeds of discord to germinate. I will do everything that prudence and integrity may dictate or permit.

I will endeavour to accommodate rather than dispute; and if this plan should fail, decent and firm representations must conclude the business of my mission.[14]

Jay, in this private manner, kept Hamilton informed on the progress of the negotiations. Their success was grave in Hamilton's estimation. War with Britain was as much to be avoided as participation in war with France. That this feat should be accomplished seemed to be of more than rational interest to him: "But this is one of those questions in which ideas of *sincerity, good faith,* and *honor,* in a relation which must always engage my particular solicitude, press my judgment to

---

[12]   *Ibid.,* 124.
[13]   John Jay to Hamilton, July 11, 1794. Johnston, *op. cit.,* 29-30.
[14]   *Ibid.*

a course of proceeding which is calculated to dispel all doubt." [15]
This statement is perhaps the most revealing and yet the most
puzzling made by Hamilton concerning the negotiations. How much
or how little he meant to say here only he and a few of his most
intimate associates would know. Certainly, his interest was more
than cursory. We know his program rested upon the maintenance of
peace and commercial intercourse, but was there a personal motive
for his active interest in the negotiations? It would be very hard to
say with the information available, and it is hardly legitimate to
admit more than this.

American foreign policy officially enunciated its neutral position
in 1793. Influential voices in the government before this time had
recommended such a course. It was a settled policy by 1794. The
nucleus of this policy in Hamilton's definition was interest. If the
interests of the United States were benefited by temporary alliances
then they were to be made; if not, they were not considered. Treaties
of alliance were quite different from treaties settling outstanding
differences between nations or from commercial treaties. The over-
tures by Denmark and Sweden to induce the United States to join in
a concert of neutral nations opposed to Britain, falls into the former
category.

Grenville's concern over the Danish-Swedish convention of neutral
nations was apparent. The Baltic states were an important source of
naval stores for Great Britain. The United States was no small con-
tributor in such items. A concert of these powers would threaten
Britain's supply. Grenville wrote Hammond that "As this is a matter
too important to admit of delay, I lose no time in giving you notice
of it and I must desire that you will exert yourself to the utmost
to prevent the American government from acceding to the measure
now proposed to them." [16] Grenville offered arguments why the
United States would not find it advantageous to enter such a convention. There was a marked difference between the actual circumstances of the United States and Denmark and Sweden, and their
interests were totally unconnected. The United States could be drawn
into an unwanted contest; the United States was surely not ignorant
"of the low and enfeebled state of the marine of both Denmark and
Sweden and how little those powers are in a condition to carry on a

---

[15] Hamilton to Washington, Cabinet Paper, June 22, 1794. Lodge, *Works*, V, 36.
[16] Lord Grenville to Hammond, May 19, 1794. F.O. 115:3, No. 12. Mayo,
Instructions, 54.

naval war against the United strength of Great Britain, Holland, Spain, and Russia and less to afford any assistance to such distant Allies as the Americans".[17]

Members of the American government were apprised of the proposed connection and immediately set out to evaluate their position. Hamilton's decisions jelled by early July 1794. He noted that a concert with Sweden and Denmark would be against the instructions of Jay. The United States enjoyed peculiar advantages from her situation which would be lost without equivalent if thrown into a common stock. Denmark and Sweden were too remote, he felt, to make cooperation useful. The entanglements of a treaty with them might be very inconvenient; the United States had better stand on her own. If war took place, common interests would secure all the cooperation practicable, and in that case occasional arrangements could be made.[18]

Hammond, in correspondence with his instructions, endeavored to ascertain the position of the American government. As was his habit, he approached Hamilton in early August, and with an indifferent appearance, suggested that reports of American accession to the neutral concert must be an idle suggestion, as such a course was inconsistent with the true interests of the United States. Hamilton, "with great seriousness and with every demonstration of sincerity", assured Hammond that it was the established policy of the United States government in every contingency, even open warfare with Britain, "to avoid entangling itself with European connexions, which could only tend to involve this country in disputes, wherein it might have no possible interest, and commit it in a common cause with allies, from whom in the moment of danger, it could derive no succour."[19] To support this, Hammond reported, Hamilton used the same arguments relied on by the British: the difference in political views between the United States and the two Baltic powers, and the inability of the latter to either protect American navigation in Europe or afford it any active assistance in its own territory. In conclusion, Hammond reminded his superiors, that in any event there was "an insuperable obstacle to any early accession on the part of the United States to this convention".[20] The Constitution precluded the president

---

[17] *Ibid.*, 55.
[18] Hamilton to Randolph, Cabinet Paper, July 8, 1794. Lodge, *Works*, V, 135-36.
[19] Hammond to Lord Grenville, Aug. 3, 1794. F.O. 5:5, No. 28. Lib. Cong.
[20] *Ibid.*

from making treaties without two-thirds concurrence of the Senate.

Hamilton's opinion was undoubtedly well founded, Grenville noted in October, but Hammond should continue to attend to the subject since Britain suspected Sweden had not dropped the project.[21] Hammond renewed his inquiries in an incidental conversation with Hamilton. Hamilton restated the opinion of the Cabinet that "in no political situation of this country, would such a measure be expedient, as it would involve it in engagements with powers, with which it can have no common interest, and from which, in the moment of difficulty or danger it would derive no benefit or assistance".[22]

America had established herself as a neutral nation. Neutrality could be effective only in its consistency. Had the United States implied she considered joining Denmark and Sweden, her national policy would have appeared at variance and her international respect would have declined appreciatively, especially in the eyes of Great Britain, at a time when both nations were in the process of negotiating. Few conceivable practical interests were served by entering the concert, a fact agreed to by Washington's advisors. Hamilton apparently thought the choice so obvious that he conceived of no primary benefit in hiding it from the British.[23] By doing so he again accus-

---

[21] Lord Grenville to Hammond, Oct. 2, 1794. F.O. 115:3, No. 19. Mayo, *Instructions*, 67.

[22] Hammond to Lord Grenville, Jan. 5, 1795. F.O. 5:8, No. 1. Lib. Cong.

[23] Lord Grenville's grave concern was already in abeyance by June 1794 when he reported to Hammond that there were indications that Denmark had not approved requesting American accession to the convention. Lord Grenville to Hammond, June 5, 1794. F.O. 115:3, No. 13. Mayo, *Instructions*, 58. Historians have indicated that Hamilton's revelations to Hammond scuttled Jay's effectiveness and America's, chances for receiving advantageous treatment of her neutral commerce and navigation; viz., Samuel Flagg Bemis, *Jay's Treaty* (New York, The MacMillan Co., 1924). It is true that Grenville's concern was lessened by Hamilton's statement, but there was no really substantial proof other than his word, that the United States would not enter the concert. Grenville was obliged to continue checking on the American position. Lord Grenville to Hammond, Oct. 3, 1794. F.O. 115:3, No. 19. *Ibid.*, 67. As to securing any real changes in the British commercial system beneficial to American neutral commerce, it was a chance in a million. Hamilton realized that Britain's safety depended upon her marine: "Her very existence as an independent power, seems to rest on a maritime superiority." "Camillus", 1795. Lodge, *Works*, V, 245. In light of this and her war with France, there would have been little hope for British recognition of American commercial proposals, i.e., free ships, free goods, if it endangered her own interests, which it would have. The Danish-Swedish convention has perhaps received an undue emphasis in evaluating the Jay-Grenville negotiations. The single most important American resource for negotiation was the fact that Britain could not afford to take on another enemy at that time; and additionally, that the American trade was important to Great Britain. It is con-

tomed the British to believing what he said and what the United States expected to do. In him the British were able to find a core of constancy. The maxim is undeniable that one who is trusted gains more insight than one who is suspected. It is a delicate equilibrium to maintain, but highly rewarding in the final consummation of a planned terminus.

It was to Hamilton that Lord Grenville again redirected his offer of British mediation in the Indian war via Hammond. Hammond was encouraged to transact confidentially with Hamilton on this most important matter. His Majesty's government was most displeased with Randolph's tactics and on more than one occasion alluded to this.

There are many Reasons for wishing that the Discussion of this important Business may, if possible, pass between you and Mr. Hamilton without any Communication of it being made to Mr. Randolph at least 'til it shall have been brought to a State in which it may be rendered public, as the whole Conduct of that Gentleman . . . has given the greatest dissatisfaction here, and particularly as with respect to the Indian War, and to the unfounded Assertions on that Subject which he has thought proper to bring forward in his Correspondence with you and to circulate through the whole of the Country by the publication of that Correspondence.[24]

Hamilton was as averse to allowing British mediation in the Indian war as were the rest of the Cabinet. He had earlier unequivocally told Hammond that the United States would not accept any such offer.[25] British mediation would subvert American independence And yet, the British still tendered their aspirations to Hamilton's ear. He seemed to have cultivated in the British a magnetic attraction to his communicative sincerity. Jefferson and Randolph riled rather than pacified, a condition which kindled a defensive attitude. Public expressions of hostility to Great Britain and favoritism to France were understandable to the British as it was "certainly very difficult for such a Government as the American to prevent these transactions".[26] But Randolph's actions went beyond this in their partisanship. Lord Grenville told Hammond that so long as such a system was followed

---

ceivable that Hamilton gained for the United States a more substantial respect and consequently greater consideration by the methods he employed, than would he have by feigning attraction to a weak cause and suggesting that the interests of the United States were opportunistic and exploitive.

[24] Lord Grenville to Hammond, Nov. 20, 1794. F.O. 115:3, No. 21. Mayo, *Instructions,* 71-73.

[25] See *ante,* 96-101.

[26] Lord Grenville to Hammond, Oct. 2, 1794. F.O. 115:3, No. 19, Mayo, *Instructions,* 68.

by those who conducted official intercourse between the two nations, it was impossible to maintain friendship and harmony. Many opportunities still remained which could be inflamed into bickerings and quarrels. It was absolutely necessary that Hammond should talk "with those Persons in America who are Friends to a System of amicable Intercourse between the Two Countries", who might convince Randolph that he must adopt a different language and conduct. If this were not feasible, at least see that he was placed in a position where his personal sentiments would not endanger the peace of the two countries.[27]

Great Britain was not a secondary power to be dealt with in an undignified and disrespectful manner. She was a powerful nation, capable of seriously threatening the future of the United States if she so chose; dignified and proud in her relations. Hamilton acknowledged Britain's stature and respected her greatness. Diplomatic relations between nations, regardless of their unequal power positions, should be professional and guided by fact and reason, not personal feelings and passions. A nation's respect was built, not fancied. It would not do to appear submissive and docile, or pretentious and pragmatical. A balance must be reached in which fraternity surmounted disagreement. These lessons Hamilton preached and practiced in America's relations with Britain. His perspicacity was much less evident in Franco-American affairs. He did not hold the French republic in high esteem and was trapped by the same perturbation which had ensnared his adversaries.

Jay affixed his signature to a treaty November 14, 1794. The treaty then returned to the United States for Senate and Presidential ratification. When the treaty became known publicly, its seemingly shaky hopes of ratification were seriously jeopardized. The nation was badly torn by factionalism and the partisans of each quickly annexed Jay's Treaty to their cause, whether pro or con. Hamilton's vital interest in retaining peace for the United States via the treaty compelled him to pacify the incendiary invectives of those seeking the failure of his stratagem. It has been seen in what capital concern Hamilton held

---

[27] Lord Grenville to Hammond, Nov. 20, 1794. F.O. 115:3, No. 22. *Ibid.*, 75. Randolph constantly took strong issue with British violations of the treaty and British depredations on American commerce. Randolph's correspondence and conversations with Great Britain appeared to them to be too partisan, and would, they felt, encourage bickerings and quarrels. British distrust was further highlighted by the diplomatic black cloud created when Randolph was charged with indiscreet disclosures to Fauchet, the French representative in the United States.

the consummation of controverted points between Britain and the United States.[28] The power of the federal government to hold the union together depended upon his financial system. The American national credit depended almost wholly on imports which a war or commercial hostility with Britain would have destroyed. From the time of Hammond's arrival in the United States Hamilton had pressed the exigency of America's needs. The immediate fear of war instigated the negotiations in 1794, but their success was measurable by Hamilton's preliminary semination of suggestions which were assimilated into the final treaty.

The fact that the treaty had been made did not insure its acceptance. Hamilton feared that the treaty would meet with opposition. In a letter to William Bradford he wrote: "I expect the treaty will labor." [29] The public furor directed against the treaty caused Hamilton to plead with the people of the United States, "that the great and cardinal *sin* of the treaty in the eyes of its adversaries is, that it puts an end to controversy with Great Britain".[30] As to any great sacrifices of American interests to Britain, nothing could be more false or ridiculous. The treaty provided satisfactorily for the great and essential controverted points between the two countries, Hamilton told his countrymen, "and only foregoes objects of an inferior and disputable nature, of no real consequence to the permanent welfare of the country".[31]

Washington admitted that he was not favorable to it: "My opinion respecting the treaty, is the same now that it was: namely, not favorable to it. . . ." [32] But his sense of duty made it incumbent that he "do what propriety, and the true interest of this country shall appear to require at my hands on so important a subject, under such delicate circumstances".[33] In this "private, and perfectly confidential" communication, Washington requested that Hamilton state the favorable and unfavorable sides of each article and compare them, so that he might see the bearing and tendency of them "and ultimately on which side the balance is to be found".[34] Washington did not want

---

[28] See *ante,* 109-11.
[29] Hamilton to William Bradford, May, 1795. Lodge, *Works,* X, 99.
[30] "Horatius", 1795. Lodge, *Works,* IV, 182.
[31] *Ibid.,* 181.
[32] Washington to the Secretary of State, July 22, 1795. Fitzpatrick, *Writings,* XXXIV, 244.
[33] Washington to Hamilton, July 3, 1795. Fitzpatrick, *Writings,* XXXIV, 277.
[34] *Ibid.*

the "opinion of *those* who were determined (before it was promulgated) to *support,* or *oppose* it . . ." for those rarely did more than
examine the side to which they leaned. "My desire is to learn from
dispassionate men, who have knowledge of the subject, and abilities
to judge of it, the genuine opinion they entertain of *each* article of
the instrument; and the *result* of it in the aggregate." [35]

Only six days from the date of this request, Hamilton returned to
Washington a thorough examination of the treaty, article by article.
His judgment of the treaty was this: it closed, as reasonably as could
be expected, the controverted points between the two countries. The
United States now, he felt, had the prospect of repossessing the
western posts, an object of primary consequence in our affairs; of
escaping implication in the European war; and, of preserving our
peace for a considerable time. The permanent articles contained
objects of real value to the United States, for the price they would
cost us in the article of compensation for debts was not in proportion
to what a single campaign would have cost to enforce our rights.
The terms of the treaty were not inconsistent with national honor.
The commercial arrangements in the temporary articles were of no
great importance either way, for they could be terminated by either
party two years after the war. Such a short duration rendered them
unimportant. Intrinsically considered, they had no very positive character of advantage or disadvantage. The commerce of the two countries would remain in all probability, as it was at present.[36]

The second article, which allowed for the return of the Western
posts in June of 1796, secured that event as far as stipulation could
do it. Hamilton felt confident that the posts would be surrendered
if the treaty was mutually ratified.

The extreme profligacy and contempt of appearances, which are implied
in the supposition of an intention to evade the surrender of the posts,
after a second and *precise* stipulation, in a treaty which adjusts all the
points of difference in a former treaty, are so palpable, that the supposition cannot be indulged without such a distrust of the faith of the
party as would forbid an attempt to treat with him.[37]

The article opened the Indian trade to the United States, relieved
the pressure of Indian wars, gave a secure course to the western

[35] *Ibid.* Hamilton was no longer a member of the Cabinet, but he continued to
advise in an unofficial capacity at Washington's request.
[36] Hamilton to Washington, Cabinet Paper, July 9, 1795. Lodge, *Works,* V,
176-77.
[37] *Ibid.,* 139.

settlements and most importantly, "it breaks up the great and dangerous project of Great Britain to confine us to the Ohio and to possess the intermediate country".[38] Finally it established the influence and authority of the government over the western country.

The third article was on the whole advantageous to the United States, according to Hamilton's assessment.[39] The British gained access to the American Indian trade which was unimportant. More importantly, the United States acquired access to theirs in Canada, which was extensive. And, because of the superior transportation facilities on the American side, the United States would be able to furnish them with European, East Indian goods and domestic articles more extensively than they could themselves. The admission of British vessels into United States rivers and mutual navigation of the Mississippi had been objected to in the article as interfering with any future regulations the United States might use to bring Britain to better commercial terms.[40] Hamilton's reply to the first objection was that it was erroneous. Regarding the Mississippi clause, it merely admitted, a positive right to navigate the river to any port which the British

[38] *Ibid.,* 140.
[39] Hamilton had indicated to Hammond that the United States would consent to grant Canadians free trade with the American Indians if Britain would grant the same right to citizens of the United States. See *ante,* 98-99.
[40] Washington was not entirely satisfied with the third article: "... the exclusion of the vessels belonging to the United States from all the 'Seaports, Harbours, Bays or Creeks of his Majesty' when theirs are admitted into ours, to the highest Ports of entry, is not marked with reciprocity ... from Quebec (but how we are to get there I know not) and upwards, the lakes, and the waters on their side of the line, are open to our commerce, and that we have equal advantages in the Indian trade on both sides; except within the limits of the Hudson's bay company.
All this looks very well on papers; but I much question whether in its operation it will not be found to work very much against us." He questioned how the United States would be able to know the limits of the Hudson Bay Company; he wondered whether British control over the Indians might foment disputes within the territories on both sides and increase the chance of Britain's securing a foothold on the Mississippi. His opinion was "that it would have been more for our peace, if not for our interest, to have restrained the traders of both nations to their own side of the line; leaving the Indians on each, to go to whichsoever their interest, convenience or inclination, might prompt them. This wd. have thwarted the views of the British on the Mississippi, whilst all the doors into upper Canada, and the Western Country would have been as wide open *then,* as they are now made by the treaty; and no difficulty, I am persuaded, would have been found by our people, of introducing Goods across the line, after they had got them to it, and the Posts possessed by us, if this avenue should be found the most convenient and cheapest." Washington to Hamilton, Private, July 13, 1795. Fitzpatrick, *Writings,* XXXIV, 238-39.

had bordering it, and a revocable right to any port the United States
had bordering it. The British would be able to use any such port in
ample a manner as they did an Atlantic port, but not in a more
ample manner. A prohibition by the United States to use any Atlantic
port would annihilate the conditional permission to go to a port on
the Mississippi. "We may, therefore, freely, as to any thing in this
article, prohibit British vessels from coming by sea from any port of
the world to the United States", he concluded.[41] The same clause,
continued Hamilton, gave permission to bring and carry into the
respective territories by land passage and inland navigation all goods
and merchandise whose importation was not entirely prohibited,
paying the duties each citizen was liable to pay.

But we may entirely prohibit any articles we please of the produce or
manufacture of Great Britain. And we may prohibit the exportation to
Great Britain of any articles whatsoever. Thus will there be ample room
to make regulations of the kind alluded to, notwithstanding any thing in
this article.[42]

The article (six) adjusting the controversy on indemnification for
losses in consequence of legal impediments for the recovery of debts,
was to be expected and entirely a part of the law or usage of nations,
noted Hamilton. Even if the United States charged Britain with
committing the first breach of the treaty, it did not follow that the
state laws impeding the recovery of debts were justifiable. Hamilton
then entered into a discussion of breach of treaty and the difficulty
of assigning the first breach. Two breaches of treaty were imputed
to Britain: the carrying away of the negroes and the retention of the
posts. "As to the first, Great Britain has much to say with truth and
justice", he felt. "Her proceedings in seducing away our negroes
during the war were to the last degree infamous, and form an in-
delible stain on her annals. But having done it, it would have been
still more infamous to have surrendered them to their masters." [43] In
his opinion, there was a well-founded doubt as to the true legal construction of the original article, for it had stipulated that Britain
remove all her armies with convenient speed without causing any
destruction or carrying away any negroes or other property. One
construction of the article could put negroes, cows, horses, and all
other property on the same footing. If negroes were subject to capture

[41] Lodge, *op. cit.*, 143.
[42] *Ibid.*, 144.
[43] Lodge, *Works*, V, 146.

in war, the captor might set them free. "If once declared free, could the grant be recalled? Could the British Government stipulate the surrender of men made free from slavery?"[44] The treaty made stipulation not to carry away, but there was no stipulation to restore. He concluded then, that "in such case, the acting of the other party, on a construction different from ours, could not be deemed such a clear manifest breach of treaty as to justify retaliation. The point was merely a matter of amicable discussion and negotiation."[45] Furthermore, if it was a breach, it was committed in 1783.

The matter of the posts was more embarrassing. The question to be settled was when they were to have been legally surrendered: from the date of the provisional or definitive treaty? The dilemma was this, said Hamilton:

that if the delay of orders for evacuating the posts till after the exchange of ratifications of the definitive treaty was a breach of the treaty ... the delay of acting upon the fifth article [for recovery of debts] till after the ratification of the definitive treaty in this country was equally a breach of the treaty on our part, and a prior, at least a contemporary, breach.[46]

As far as Hamilton could surmise, the first breach was made by the United States. However, even admitting the first breaches by Britain, it would have been

dishonorable and unjust in us to have interfered with the recovery of private debts; it was dishonorable and unjust to have interfered with them on the gronds which were the pretexts, and it is honorable and just to make compensation. The reputation of the country as well as its peace required the stipulation.[47]

The seventh article dealt with indemnification for captures of American vessels. "Indemnification on equitable principles was all that could be expected", Hamilton estimated.[48] The United States could not have demanded a gross sum because there was no standard by which to ascertain what was proper. For this reason, Britain could not be expected to agree to a gross sum. "This is not the way that nations deal with each other unless where one is in a situation to dictate to the other. This was not our situation."[49] The article was as well arranged as could be expected.

44 *Ibid.*, 148.
45 *Ibid.*, 148-49.
46 *Ibid.*, 150.
47 *Ibid.*, 155.
48 *Ibid.*, 156.
49 *Ibid.*

The first ten articles were permanent. Hamilton's verdict on them was that they closed the various matters of controversy with Britain reasonably. The question of compensation for negroes was of no great moment, for it involved no principle of future operation. It had been a point of doubtful right and by this treaty it terminated in itself. The actual pecuniary value, he stated, in a national sense was inconsiderable and insignificant.[50]

The commercial portion of the treaty was contained in the remaining articles, which were temporary. If the twelfth article were accepted, the duration of the treaty was to be twelve years. Without the twelfth, the commercial part of the treaty would expire in two years after the end of the present war. The eleventh article introduced the following articles. The twelfth became the source of violent vituperation, for it concerned a matter of vital interest to Hamilton and his countrymen, the West India trade. The article granted a limited privilege of entry into the West Indies, in American vessels of no more than seventy tons, but prevented exportation of molasses, sugar, coffee or cotton from the United States. The restraints placed on American exportations of West Indian products, would have cut off the re-exportation not only of British but of French and all foreign West Indian products. "This article", said Hamilton, "is in my judgment an exceptionable one".[51] Had the restriction been confined to articles from the British Islands, it would have been justified. The fact that the restriction extended to both articles from other countries and to ones which were the growth of the United States, made the article inadmissible from the beginning. A restriction upon anything not the produce of the treaty itself, was unprecedented and wrong. Furthermore, it might prove a source of dissatisfaction to France, "and though I would not omit any measure which I thought for the national interest", he said, "because any foreign power might capriciously dislike it, yet I would do no act giving a reasonable cause of dissatisfaction." [52] For these reasons, he was glad that the Senate had refused to accept it, even at the risk of the treaty. Though Jay's reasoning that it was important to establish the precedent of a breach in the navigation system of Britain by formal treaty [53] was right, it was outweighed by other considerations, Hamilton deduced.[54]

[50]   *Ibid.*, 162.
[51]   *Ibid.*
[52]   *Ibid.*, 162-63.
[53]   Jay to Edmund Randolph, Nov. 19, 1794. Johnston, *op. cit.*, IV, 142.
[54]   Hamilton suggested a modification for the twelfth article: extend the tonnage

The thirteenth article was valuable because it converted into a right by stipulation the most essential and extensive parts of what the United States previously enjoyed by mere sufferance of the local government in the British East Indies. "The treaty, though it permits a circuitous trade to India, permits only a direct trade from India to the United States; but when the articles arrive within the United States, we may re-export them, or do whatever else we please." [55] To Hamilton the article was all on one side and favorable to the United States.[56]

The treaty established reciprocally the rule of the most favored nation (Article 15). "It was impossible to expect that a treaty could be formed of which this was not the basis", said Hamilton.[57] The article declared that there would be no prohibition on the exportation or importation from the respective territories of the contracting parties which was not equally extended to all other nations. "This permits us to carry to the British dominions any article the growth or manufacture of another country, which may be carried from such country to those dominions. This is a serious innovation on the British navigation act, and an important privilege to us." [58]

Regarding the article (seventeen) recognizing the right of a belligerent nation to take its enemy's goods out of neutral ships, it was "impossible to deny that the principle recognized is conformable with the laws of nations".[59] He discussed the principle that free ships made free goods. The United States had early in her political life given up, by unanimous opinion, such ground as untenable. The

---

(90 tons would be advantageous) and restrain the prohibition to export from the United States, to articles of the growth or production of the British West Indies. "The more the tonnage is extended the better. ... I had even rather have the article with seventy, as it stood, than not at all, if the restriction on exportation is placed on the proper footing." Hamilton to Washington, Sept. 4, 1795. Lodge, *Works*, VII, 202.

[55]   Lodge, *Works*, V, 163.
[56]   Hamilton felt a valuable alteration, if it were possible, would be a stipulated right for "the United States to go with articles taken in the British territories in India to other parts of Asia". The limitation placed upon the United States to carry only to America was probably to prevent American interference in the European trade in India goods of the British East India Company. "If so, there could be no objection to our having a right to carry commodities from the British territories to other parts of Asia." If this latitude could not be obtained, the right to carry to China would be a great gain. Lodge, *Works*, VI, 203.
[57]   Lodge, *Works*, V, 166.
[58]   *Ibid.*, 178.
[59]   *Ibid.*, 166.

President's files of Jefferson's letters gave proof of this. It was not probable that the principle would ever become an established law of nations for it was contrary to the spirit and actions of war. The dilemma was to renounce a pretension of the principle, or insist upon it and maintain it. In Hamilton's estimation, to have insisted upon it would have been madness, for a young and weak nation could not take a stand which was not clearly maintained on precedent and principle.[60]

Enumeration of articles of contraband was dealt with in the eighteenth article. Hamilton indicated that he would have liked the treaty better without this article, for it possibly could "become the pretext of abuses on the side of Great Britain, and of complaint on that of France. . . . On the whole, I think this article the worst in the treaty, except the twelfth, though not defective enough to be an objection to its adoption." [61] The remaining articles were generally acceptable, Hamilton concluded, for they were becoming formulas in most modern treaties.

Charges that the treaty was inconsistent with treaties with other powers, Hamilton answered in this way. A comparison of previous commercial treaties with this one would leave the advantage with the earlier ones. The footing would remain essentially equal respecting European dominions of the different powers. As to their colonies, Britain by its treaty with the United States, gave the United States in this treaty greater advantages than any other nation having colonies. "There is nothing in any of our other treaties equivalent to the advantages to us in the British East Indies", he noted.[62] To this could be added the advantages of the Canada article. The stipulations that free ships make free goods and the enumeration of articles of contraband were provisions which American experience in the present war in reference to France had shown were not advantages to be counted

---

[60]   *Ibid.*, 167-68.

[61]   *Ibid.*, 171. Hamilton considered the article an "unpleasant one". Although he thought there was little chance of altering it for the better "it may be necessary, for the justification of the President, to attempt it". The standard to be approached was that found in the French treaty. "As to the point of free ships making free goods, though it be desirable to us to establish it if practicable — and it ought to be aimed at — yet I neither expect that it will be done at present, nor that the *great maritime powers* will be disposed to suffer it to become an established rule, and I verily believe that it will be very liable, though stipulated, to be disregarded, as it has been by France through the greater part of the present war." Lodge, *Works*, VI, 204.

[62]   Lodge, *Works*, V, 178-79.

upon. Since the permanent articles were of material consequence
and the temporary ones of small importance, since American faith
was preserved with other powers and no improper concessions had
been admitted on our part, Hamilton concluded that it was in the
interest of the United States to allow the treaty to go into effect.

Did the treaty give umbrage to France? Only if France were un-
reasonable, said Hamilton. American engagements with her remained
unimpaired and France remained on as good a footing as Britain. He
noted that:

We are in a deplorable situation if we cannot secure our peace, and
promote our interests, by means which not only do not derogate from
our faith, but which leave the same advantages to France as to other
powers with whom we form treaties. Equality is all that can be claimed
for us. It is improbable that France will take umbrage, because there
is no disposition on her part to break with us, and because her situation
forbids a breach.[63]

Would our treaty with Britain hinder making a more beneficial treaty
with France, Hamilton asked? "This can only turn upon the question
of equivalents to be given by us. . . . But it would be very unwise to
refrain from doing with one power, a thing which it was our interest
to do, because there was a *possibility* that some other might be
willing to make a better bargain with us." [64] France had given the
United States no evidence of willingness to make a better bargain.
All she had proffered was that the United States become party to
the war. "As she will and ought to calculate her own interest, we
ought to dismiss the expectation of peculiar favors. Favors, indeed,
in trade, are very absurd, and generally imaginary things." [65] He
urged that the United States remember "that the short necessary
duration of our treaty leaves us a wide field future and not remote".[66]

Hamilton publicly defended Jay's Treaty as Camillus in a series
of articles beginning in July of 1795 and carrying over into 1796.
Although these were of greater length than his private examination
of the treaty for Washington, the "Camillus" publications were essentially founded on the same arguments. The technique of turning to
the people as an important fount of opinion was not new to Hamilton. He had at a very early stage in his public career introduced his
thoughts to the people, always with great success. One of the best

63 *Ibid.*
64 *Ibid.*, 180.
65 *Ibid.*
66 *Ibid.*

examples of the hegemonic persuasiveness of his written word can be seen in his defense of the Federal Constitution in *The Federalist*. The fact that he appealed to the public on more than one important occasion would indicate that he was aware no policy could succeed unless it had national opinion behind it.[67] The shrewdness of his political genius suggested a program of domestic propaganda which his pen masterfully created.

As Camillus, Hamilton divulged the trenchant expedience of the treaty for the United States. It was his opinion that because "of the situation of the thing, and of the parties, there never could be a rational doubt that the compromising plan was the only one on which the United States and Great Britain could ever terminate their differences without war. . . ."[68] The calamities of war were many. American trade, navigation and mercantile capital would be destroyed. Since Spain was an associate of England, a general Indian war might be expected which would lay desolate the whole frontier. With our exports obstructed, agriculture would languish and all other industries would proportionately suffer. The public debt would be greatly augmented, and with it would come a large increase of taxes and burdens on the people.[69] It was in the interest of the United States to "exert all our prudence and address to keep out of war as long as it should be possible; to defer, to a state of manhood, a struggle to which infancy is ill adapted".[70] Why? "If there be a foreign power which sees with envy or ill-will our growing prosperity, that power must discern that our infancy is the time for clipping our wings. We ought to be wise enough to see that this is not a time for trying our strength."[71]

Hamilton estimated that once our disputes with Britain were terminated and we escaped the storm agitating Europe, "we may hope to postpone war to a distant period".[72] Only one power would remain with which the United States had any embarrassing questions: Spain and the question of the Mississippi.

---

[67] Hamilton reminded Wolcott: "Remember always as a primary motive of action, that the favourable opinion of our country is to be secured." Gibbs, *op. cit.*, 360. He told Rufus King that "we must seize and carry along with us the public opinion and loss of time may be loss of everything". Hamilton to Rufus King, April 15, 1796. Lodge, *Works*, X, 157.

[68] "Camillus", 1795. Lodge, *Works*, V, 213.

[69] *Ibid.*, 202.

[70] *Ibid.*, 207.

[71] *Ibid.*

[72] *Ibid.*

How unwise would it have been to invite or facilitate a quarrel with Great Britain at a moment when she and Spain were engaged in a common cause, both of them having, besides, controverted points with the United States! How wise will it be to adjust our differences with the most formidable of these two powers, and to have only to contest with one of them![73]

He was persuaded that "In all questions between us and Great Britain, honor permitted the moderate course..."[74] In those questions regarding failure to execute the peace treaty, there were undoubtedly mutual faults, and therefore a case for negotiation and mutual reparation. The injuries suffered and complained of by the United States in the present war were also negotiable, for the first rested on a controverted point in the laws of nations. "The second left open the question, whether the principal injury was a designed act of the government or a misconstruction of its courts."[75] If the United States had gone to war as was recommended, she would not have followed the admonitions of honor, but would have submitted to the impulse of passion and frenzy. Was war the alternative to negotiation, Hamilton asked? Yes, he answered, that or disgrace. Britain and the United States had been brought to issue: spoliations on American commerce, the evils of a protracted Indian war, the retention of the western posts designs to contract our boundaries, obstruction of American settlements and the enjoyment of private rights produced growing discontent in the west. These issues made it indispensable that there should be a settlement of these differences and a reparation of new wrongs, Hamilton said, "or, that the sword should vindicate our rights".[76]

Why, if the United States suffered under the duress of such wrongs, should she attempt to negotiate instead of declaring war? Hamilton indicated a number of important considerations. Forces opposing the treaty charged that the United States had prostrated herself before Great Britain when that power was in a vulnerable and weak position. Any such picture of Britain as a prostrate nation was exaggerated and false, Hamilton insisted. No one could deny that Britain was triumphant on the ocean and that her acquisitions thus far were greater than those which France had made. She owed an immense debt, but she possessed an immense credit, which gave no indication of being impaired. Even though British credit had be-

[73]   *Ibid.*, 207-08.
[74]   *Ibid.*, 237.
[75]   *Ibid.*
[76]   *Ibid.*, 240-41.

come an article of faith and not reason in the British mind, it was evident that it still afforded prodigious resources, and would continue to do so for some time to come.[77] British manufactures were still in a comparatively flourishing condition and her foreign commerce continued to be immense. A critical view of Britain in her foreign connections would not substantiate a charge of exhaustion, Hamilton found. Her allies included the two greatest powers of Europe, excepting France: that is, Russia and Austria. Spain and Sardinia made common cause with her. France evidently seemed unable to annoy Russia, and could not make further acquisitions in Austria because of her geographical position. As long as Britain maintained a decided maritime superiority, she and her possessions were essentially safe. Even supposing her abandoned by her allies, she could never be in the position described by the opposers of the treaty. If British allies were fatigued and exhausted, France could be in no better condition. In fact, France was probably more fatigued and exhausted than her adversaries.[78] Hamilton concluded his refutation of the supposed vulnerability of Great Britain by saying: "This fair comparison of the relative situation of the contending parties will, I know, be stigmatized as blazoning the strength and resources of Great Britain, and depreciating the advantages of France. But the cant phrases of party cannot alter the nature of truth. . . ."[79]

What would it have meant to the United States had she threatened a policy of confiscation and sequestration of private property? Would it have prevented war, Hamilton wondered? There was no indication that such a practice would avoid war, but another reaction should be predicted.

The storms of war occur so suddenly and so often, as to forbid the supposition, that the merchants of our country would trust their property, to any extent, or for any duration, in another country, which was in the practice of confiscating or sequestering the effects of its enemies, found within its territories, at the commencement of a war. That practice, therefore, would necessarily paralyze and wither the commerce of the country in which it obtained.[80]

The pretension of such a right would have a most inimical aspect towards commerce and credit. Hamilton examined the effects for Britain and the United States. Great Britain lacked good sense if she

[77] *Ibid.* 256-57.
[78] *Ibid.*, 259.
[79] *Ibid.*, 262.
[80] Lodge, *Works,* V, 444-45.

failed to see that by making war on the United States she made war upon her own merchants. Depredations on American trade destroyed those resources from which they were to be paid. The animating principle of American foreign commerce from the first settlement had been the credit our merchants were able to obtain abroad, and especially in Great Britain. Every merchant knew and felt this, and was sensible that the case would continue the same for many years to come. "This, in our situation", Hamilton felt, "is a peculiar reason, of the utmost force, for renouncing the pretension in question".[81] To exercise it or threaten to, would have one of two effects. It would either deprive our merchants of the credit so important to them, or oblige them to pay a premium for it proportionate to the amount of risk. Speaking even more truthfully, it would combine the two effects: credit would be cramped and what was given would be subject to a high premium. The United States would be paying exorbitantly for a pretension of little value in the operation of her trade. The principle could never be exercised in the United States without great and lasting mischief.[82]

Hamilton's arguments demonstrated the value of moderation, in that having pursued it, peace had been preserved and the differences between both nations satisfactorily settled. The matter of the negroes

was too questionable in point of right, too insignificant in point of interest, to have been suffered to be an impediment to the immense objects which were to be promoted by an accommodation of differences acceptable in other respects. There was no general principle of national right of policy to be renounced. No consideration of honor forbade the renunciation: every calculation of interest invited to it.[83]

British renunciation of the posts was of immense value to the United States in Hamilton's viewpoint:

... the possession of those posts by us has an intimate connection with the preservation of union between our Western and Atlantic territories. ... Is there anything in the treaty conceded by us to Great Britain, to be placed in competition with this single acquisition? The answer could not fail [Hamilton stated] to be in the negative.[84]

Moreover, the United States had "never appeared so august and respectable as in the position which is assumed. ... Europe was struck

---

81 *Ibid.*
82 *Ibid.*, 449-55.
83 *Ibid.*, 240.
84 *Ibid.*, 255.

with the dignified moderation of our conduct; and the character of our government and nation acquired a new elevation." [85]

In 1801 Hamilton reminded the Electors of the State of New York of the extravagant predictions made against the *"British Treaty"*. He asked them in what way had they been realized?

You have seen our peace preserved, you have seen our western posts surrendered, your commerce proceed with success in its wonted channels, and our agriculture flourish to the extent of every reasonable wish; and you have been witnesses to none of the mischiefs which were foretold. You will, then, conclude with us that the clamors against this treaty are the mere ebullitions of ignorance, of prejudice, and of faction.[86]

With the ratification of Jay's Treaty, Hamilton's major objectives were accomplished. In 1783 the United States had become a new nation by virtue of the peace treaty. Hamilton envisaged an independent and respected place for the United States among nations, and the young country's future had to be built upon a lasting foundation. Hamilton's concept of such a foundation was to be a commercial one, as we have seen. The leading commercial nation of the world and the nation withholding full performance of the Anglo-American peace treaty was Great Britain. It was more these conditions than the participants which were pertinent to Hamilton's plans. Between 1783 and 1795 he endeavored to cultivate the former or commercial relations, and settle the latter or treaty violations. Jay's Treaty climaxed these efforts.

---

[85] *Ibid.*, 205.
[86] Address to the Electors of the State of New York, 1801. Lodge, *Works*, VIII, 238.

CHAPTER VII

THE FRENCH ISSUE

Jay's Treaty tranquillized and pacified Anglo-American differences. The polemic after 1796 was between France and the United States. Hamilton had resigned from office in 1795, but he continued to participate actively in the business of the government. His capacity was more than advisory; he actually guided much of the progress of American foreign relations from 1796 through 1800. These relations were primarily with France, but they bear a remarkable resemblance to prior Anglo-American difficulties.

As Hamilton resided at a distance from the seat of government, much of his advice was recorded in his own hand. His records of the events following Jay's Treaty are decidedly more revealing in the scope of his role than are his records of American disputes with Great Britain. We may surmise that his participation in the affairs of the United States as Secretary of the Treasury and a member of the cabinet, was probably to a great extent oral. He was involved in the thick of the English controversy. Conversely, during the French crisis, he offered his services by letter as a private citizen. Furthermore, there is no reason to assume that his policies would have changed. One of the major qualities of Hamilton's thought was its consistency. The French crisis may offer valuable clues for Hamilton's British orientation of American foreign policy. The following words suggest this possibility:

As in the case of England, so now, my opinion is to exhaust the expedient of negotiation, and at the same time to prepare vigorously for the worst. This is sound policy.[1]

You will perceive that the general plan is analogous to what was done in the case of Great Britain, though there are faults in the detail. Some

[1] Hamilton to Oliver Wolcott, March 30, 1797. Gibbs, *Memoirs of the Administrations of Washington and John Adams, edited from the papers of Oliver Wolcott, Secretary of the Treasury* (New York, William Van Norden, 1846), I, 485.

people cannot learn that the only force which befits a government is in the *thought* and *action*, not in *words*, and many reverse the golden rule.[2]

I take the liberty to express to you my opinion that it is of the true policy as well as of the dignity of our government, to act with spirit and energy as well toward Great Britain as France. I would *mete* the same measure to both of them, though it should ever furnish the extraordinary spectacle of a nation at war with two nations at war with each other. One of them would quickly court us, and by this course of conduct our citizens will be enthusiastically united to the government. It will evince that we are neither *Greeks* nor *Trojans*. In very crititcal cases bold expedients are often necessary.[3]

Hamilton's earliest references to France were during the American Revolution. His comments bespoke the assurance of a great power in their connotation. When the United States was transacting a foreign loan with France in 1780, Hamilton wrote that "The most effectual way will be to tell France that without it we must make terms with Great Britain. This must be done with plainness and firmness; but with respect, and without petulance; not as a menace, but as a candid declaration of our circumstances." [4] The evidence for relying on such a course was his evaluation of French incentives. "We need not fear to be deserted by France. Her interest and honor are too deeply involved in our fate, and she can make no possible compromise." [5]

When France became our ally, Hamilton suggested a certain practicality in the forces motivating their alliance to the United States. France was undoubtedly interested in our success, he thought. They were willing to give the United States every aid essential to our preservation. It was natural, however, that such aid would be given with as much convenience to themselves as was possible. He apprehended that France was not overfond of plunging into war with Britain if she could avoid it and still answer the end she pursued. The United States could conclude that France would not force England into a war unless she found our affairs absolutely required it, and England would not enter into war until she was compelled to.[6] The implication became explicit in 1793. The American Revolution early attracted the notice of France, Hamilton told his readers. Prior

---

[2] Hamilton to Rufus King, June 6, 1797. Lodge, *Works*, X, 266-67.
[3] Hamilton to Timothy Pickering, June 8, 1798. Lodge, *Works*, X, 294.
[4] Hamilton to James Duane, Sept. 3, 1780. Lodge, *Works*, I, 229.
[5] *Ibid.*
[6] Hamilton to Dr. Hugh Knox, July 1777. Lodge, *Works*, IX, 86.

to the acknowledgement of American independence, any aid given by France "wore the appearance rather of a desire to keep alive disturbances which might embarrass a rival, than of a serious design to assist a revolution, or a serious expectation that it could be effected".[7] Not until American victories at Saratoga were the hesitations of France decided. "The dismemberment of this country from Great Britain was an obvious and a very important interest of France. It cannot be doubted that it was both the determining motive and an adequate compensation for the assistance afforded to us." [8]

Hamilton referred consistently to French interests as the source of her motivation toward America. There are few instances, if any, in which he refers to British interests. However, this is weak support for any contention that he was obsessed with French motives of self-interest and excepted British self-interest, for he often established the policies of his own country on self-interest.

At the time of the Proclamation of Neutrality Hamilton discussed why the United States was not obligated to join France in fending off her enemies. The primary reason he found was that our treaty with her was a defensive one; French actions were offensive in nature. "France, it is certain, was the first to declare war against every one of the Powers with which she is at war. Whether she had good cause or not, therefore, in each instance, the war is completely *offensive* on her part." [9] And so, he said, the doctrines of writers, the practice of nations, and the dictates of reason supported the principle that whenever one nation adopted a conduct which tended to disturb the tranquillity and established order of its neighbors, or manifested a spirit of self-aggrandizement, it was lawful for other nations to combine against it and by force to control the effects of those maxims and spirit. French conduct, calmly and impartially viewed, was an offence against nations and should be checked.[10]

Hamilton's attitude toward French actions was less than tolerant. The French Revolution may have originally sought to propagate liberty, although Hamilton did not see that that sentiment had existed with reference to French interest in the American Revolution. "It is certain that the love of liberty was not a national sentiment in France when a zeal for our cause first appeared among that people." [11]

[7] "Pacificus", 1793. Lodge, *Works*, IV, 466.
[8] Lodge, *Works*, IV, 467.
[9] Hamilton to Washington, Cabinet Paper, May 2, 1793. Lodge, *Works*, IV, 398.
[10] *Ibid.*, 406-07.
[11] "Pacificus", 1793. Lodge, *Works*, IV, 472.

Comparison of the two revolutions was also irreconcilable to him. It would be dangerous and inconvenient to our interests if the nations of Europe were impressed with the idea that the United States was actuated by the same spirit which misguided the affairs of France. Some had compared the French cause with America in her revolution. Hamilton did not:

> Would to Heaven we could discern in the mirror of French affairs the same humanity, the same decorum, the same gravity the same order, the same dignity, the same solemnity, which distinguished the cause of the American Revolution. Clouds and darkness would not then rest upon the issue as they now do.[12]

According to Hamilton, the United States did not really owe anything to France. If the organ of the nation granting us aid acted from unworthy motives irrelative to our advantage, or from a base speculation, he argued, and if afterwards it showed a hostile temper to the confirmation of American prosperity and security, that organ either acquired no title to our gratitude in the first instance or forfeited it in the second.[13] Nothing was to be gained by going to war. France was singly engaged against the greatest part of Europe; ". . . she has but one enemy, and that is all of Europe." [14] Her internal affairs were in disorder and her navy inconsiderable. The United States had a greater interest in preserving peace than in any advantages which France might use to tempt our participation. Commercial privileges were of real value in our estimation, but even a carte blanche on these by France would be an inadequate recompense for renouncing peace and committing the United States to the chances of a precarious and perilous war. If the commercial privileges conceded were not founded in a real, permanent, and mutual interest, of what value would the treaty be, he asked? It was better to trust "that commercial privileges, which are truly founded in mutual interest, will grow out of that interest, without the necessity of giving a premium for them at the expense of our peace?" [15] As there was little advantage in being tied to France, Hamilton explained away the legal bonds by reasoned argument. However, the peace treaty of 1783 with Britain was another matter; it was obligatory. British troops and agents were oper-

---

[12]   Hamilton to [receiver of this letter is not known], May 1793. Lodge, *Works*, X, 44-45.
[13]   "Pacificus", 1793. Lodge, *Works*, IV, 479.
[14]   *Ibid.*, 478.
[15]   "Pacificus", 1793. Lodge, *Works*, IV, 485. These are interesting questions when applied to Hamilton's instructions in the Jay mission.

ating in our interior and Britain commanded the seas. There were good reasons in his estimation for complying with that treaty.

Hamilton saw an instructive lesson for the people of the United States in French machinations of 1793. "It ought to teach us not to overrate foreign friendships, and to be upon our guard against foreign attachments." [16] Foreign friendships would generally be hollow and delusive, and foreign attachments would have a natural tendency to lead the United States from her true interest making us dupes of foreign influence. Both would serve to introduce a principle which was anti-national in its effect. "Foreign influence", he said, "is truly the Grecian horse to a republic. We cannot be too careful to exclude its entrance." [17]

French partisans in America and France herself charged that Jay's Treaty abridged Franco-American treaty rights. Although French violations of American neutral rights increased, her faithful partisans continued to hanker after a French connection, or at least a more grateful attitude. Hamilton's answer to these suggestions was precise: "You ought to spurn from you, as the box of Pandora, the fatal heresy of a close alliance ... with France. This would at once make you a mere satellite of France, and entangle you in all the contests, broils, and wars of Europe." [18]

French depredations were equal to any suffered under British measures, Hamilton insisted. The real motives of French abridgement of neutral rights was to destroy British commerce, and in that way extinguish the sources of her revenue and credit, disable her from continuing in the war, and compel her to accept any condition of peace.[19] "And here we find the true solution of those unfriendly proceedings, on the part of France toward this country, which are hypocritically charged to the account of the treaty with Great Britain, and other acts of pretended infidelity in our government." [20] The indiscriminate spoliation of the commerce of neutral powers was proof that France was actuated by a general plan of policy, Hamilton

---

[16]   *Ibid.*, 481.
[17]   "Pacificus", 1793. Lodge, *Works*, IV, 481.
[18]   "Horatius", 1795. Lodge, *Works*, IV, 184.
[19]   Hamilton expressed it in another way: "The conduct of France towards Great Britain is the copy of that of Rome towards Carthage. Its manifest aim is to destroy the principal obstacle to a domination over Europe. History proves that Great Britain has repeatedly upheld the balance of power there, in opposition to the grasping ambition of France." "The Stand", 1798. Lodge, *Works*, VI, 282.
[20]   "The Warning", 1797. Lodge, *Works*, VI, 231.

charged.[21] Some pretext was necessary, and France chose allegations of discontent with the United States.

It was said, Hamilton noted, that the treatment received from France was no worse than that which we received from Britain. The apology, even if founded in fact, was a miserable subterfuge, he felt. "For what excuse is it to France, or what consolation to us, that she, our boasted friend and benefactress, treats us only not worse than a power which is stigmatized as an envious rival and an implacable foe?"[22] The truth was that the United States never did tolerate the aggressions of Great Britain; we had resisted them steadily and with success. Using armed negotiation, seconded by an embargo, we sent to demand a revocation of orders and retribution for losses. Because of this policy,

the redress obtained from Great Britain was a principal cause of the happy accommodation of our dispute with Spain, and the recognition of our right to navigate the Mississippi, and of the establishment of a southern boundary equal to our most sanguine wishes. These are the fruits (and immense fruits they are) of a vigorous though temperate resistance to the aggressions of Great Britain.[23]

Any accusations that the American government permitted Britain to do as France was doing were false, he concluded.

France had an "indisputable title to the culpable pre-eminence of having taken the lead in the violation of neutral rights".[24] Britain had allowed United States trade with France in all articles, except corn, flour and meal, and contraband articles to go unmolested. He commented:

Iniquitous and oppressive as were the acts of Great Britain, how very far short do they fall of the more iniquitous and oppressive decrees of France, as these have been construed and acted upon, not only by the colonial administrations, but by some of its tribunals in Europe![25]

Only one conclusion could be drawn: long before the American treaty with England, French vexations of American trade in French ports

[21] Hamilton had prophesied this policy earlier: "If the war of Europe continues, the efforts of France will be likely to be levelled as a primary object against the commerce and credit of Great Britain; and to injure these, she may think it advisable to make war upon our trade — forgetting perhaps that the consequence may be to turn it more entirely into the channels of Great Britain." Hamilton to Rufus King, Dec. 16, 1796. Lodge, *Works*, X, 215.

[22] "The Warning", 1797. Lodge, *Works*, VI, 245.

[23] *Ibid.*, 247.

[24] *Ibid.*, 254.

[25] *Ibid.*, 256.

had become intolerable. In Hamilton's words: "... the predatory system of France existed before the treaty, and has only of late acquired greater activity from the cravings of an exhausted treasury." [26]

Jay's Treaty was being used as a pretense for ill treatment, he deduced, as were all other allegations. The President would have to make a final appeal to the justice and "insist in mild but explicit terms on the renunciation of the pretension to intercept the lawful commerce of neutrals with the enemies of France.... If the experiment shall fail", he said, "there will be nothing left but to repel aggression and defend our commerce and independence". [27]

Hamilton was deeply concerned that the United States could not avert war with France. He was perhaps less sure that we would avoid war in the case of France than he had been with Britain, for he emphasized several times both the seriousness of the occasion and the importance of convincing the people and the enemies of the government [28] that the administration had done everything in its power. There was no doubt in his mind, however, that war must be opposed. "The present is, in my opinion, as critical a situation as our government has been in; requiring all its prudence, all its wisdom, all its moderation, all its firmness." [29] He warned Washington that the card to be played was perhaps the most delicate that had occurred in their administration, for nations as individuals sometimes got into squabbles from a manner more than the matter of their relations. It was all-important if possible to avoid a rupture with France, but if that could not be, "to evince to the people that there has been an unequivocal disposition to avoid it". [30] To Theodore Sedgwick he

[26] *Ibid.*, 259.
[27] *Ibid.*, 237.
[28] He wrote William Smith that "We seem now to feel and reason as the *Jacobins* did when Great Britain insulted and injured us, though certainly we have at least as much need of a temperate conduct now as we had then." Hamilton to William Smith, April 10, 1797. Lodge, *Works*, X, 256.

There is evidence that Hamilton gave great weight to the powers of the "enemies of the government" and what their program meant to the future of the United States. He wrote Washington that "it is more and more evident that the powerful faction which has for years opposed the government, is determined to go every length with France ... they are ready to *new-model* our Constitution under the *influence* or *coercion* of France, to form with her a perpetual alliance, *offensive* and *defensive*, and to give her a monopoly of our trade by *peculiar* and *exclusive* privileges. This would be in substance ... to make this country a province of France." Hamilton to Washington, May 19, 1798. *Ibid.*, 284-85.
[29] Hamilton to Oliver Wolcott, Nov. 22, 1796. Gibbs, *op. cit.*, I, 398.
[30] Hamilton to Washington, Nov. 5, 1796. Lodge, *Works*, X, 200.

allowed it was in America's interest to preserve peace, but if we could not, "it will be very important to prove that no endeavor to do it has been omitted".[31] He made no apology for offering Timothy Pickering, the Secretary of State, his opinion: "I look upon the question before the public as nothing less than whether we shall maintain our independence; and I am prepared to do it in every event, and at every hazard." [32]

Hamilton as much as told his correspondents what to do in every instance. The facility with which he did so, and the ease in which his colleagues embraced the advice, suggest that he and they were used to such a process. The same situation may well have existed while Hamilton was Secretary of the Treasury; different in only one aspect, that is, oral communication was available. His directions in matters involving France were very explicit. This may have been because he could not personally handle the problem, as he had with Britain.

His advice regarding France resembled that which he had given and used to settle Anglo-American differences.

Our discussions, therefore, ought to be *calm, smooth,* inclined to be argumentative; when remonstrance and complaint are unavoidable, carrying into the face of them a *reluctance* and *regret,* mingling a steady assertion of our rights and adherence to principle with the language of moderation, and, as long as it can be done, of friendship.[33]

The maintenance of peace was still vitally important in his estimation. "The *estimation* of the merit of all our past measures depends on the final preservation of peace. This, besides the interest of the country in peace, is a very powerful reason for attempting every thing." [34]

The United States would have to negotiate. Hamilton's idea was to send an extraordinary mission to France. "As an imitation of what was done in the case of Great Britain, it will argue to the people equal solicitude. To France it will have a similar aspect ... and will in some degree soothe her pride." [35] He would accumulate proofs of French violence and demonstrate to the public that every possible effort had been made to preserve peace.

[31] Hamilton to Theodore Sedgwick, Feb. 26, 1797. *Ibid.*, 239.
[32] Hamilton to Timothy Pickering, March 17, 1798. *Ibid.*, 275-76.
[33] Hamilton to Washington, Nov. 5, 1796. Lodge, *Works*, X, 200.
[34] Hamilton to Timothy Pickering, March 29, 1797. *Ibid.*, 247.
[35] Hamilton to Washington, Jan. 22, 1797. Lodge, *Works*, X, 233-34.

The idea is a plausible one, that as we sent an Envoy Extraordinary to Britain, so we ought to send one to France. . . . These and other reasons (and principally to avoid rupture with a political monster, which seems destined soon to have no competitor but England) make me even anxious for an extraordinary mission.[36]

What should be the powers of the commissioners? To adjust compensations amicably and revise and remodify the political and commercial relations of the two countries. They should endeavor to get rid of the mutual guaranty in the treaty, or, if that was impracticable, to stipulate specific succors in lieu of it. The *casus foederis* should be defined "to be that case, in which the first act of actual hostility by Sea or land is committed against the ally. . . ."[37] It would also be expedient to tell France that if there was anything in the British treaty which she wished to incorporate in her treaty with the United States, the United States was ready to do so, "having no wish to give any other power privileges which France may not equally enjoy on the same terms".[38] Respecting commercial agreements, he advised that "In general it is wisest neither to *give* nor take peculiar privileges — but equalize our commercial system with all nations."[39] It would be very difficult to make articles which did not interfere with other treaties. France could be favored by stipulating "that certain articles of *her production or manufacture,* not common to Great Britain, which enter largely into our possessions should be admitted without duty, or on light duties to be specified".[40] The subject was better avoided, he thought, for "The diminution of our Revenue and jealousies in other powers will be certain evils, for which France will & can give no real equivalent."[41]

American duty, honor, and safety required that vigorous and comprehensive measures of defence be taken while still leaving the door to accommodation open, he demanded. This would include measures "adequate to the immediate protection of our commerce, to the security of our ports, and to our eventual defence in cases of invasion. . . ."[42] An attitude of calm defiance suited Hamilton. Congress

---

[36] Hamilton to William Smith, April 5, 1797. *Ibid.,* 253-54.
[37] Hamilton to James McHenry, undated. Steiner, *op. cit.,* 220.
[38] Hamilton to James McHenry, undated. Steiner, *The Life and Correspondence of James McHenry,* 219.
[39] *Ibid.,* 220.
[40] *Ibid.*
[41] *Ibid.,* 221.
[42] Hamilton to Timothy Pickering, March 17, 1798. Lodge, *Works,* X, 276.

should lay an embargo, revenues should be increased vigorously, and naval forces provided for convoying. A provisional army of 25,000 men should be formed and the cavalry and artillery increased. He told both James McHenry, the Secretary of War, and Timothy Pickering, they were to "do as much of all this as you can. Make a last effort for peace, but be prepared for the worst".[43] He warned them that "In this time of general convulsion, in a state of things which threatens all civilization, 'tis a great folly to wrap ourselves up in a cloak of security." [44]

What were Hamilton's real motives? What did he hope to gain for the United States out of the French crisis? He told Oliver Wolcott, his successor as Secretary of the Treasury, that the French alliance "in its future operation must be against our interest. The door to escape from it is opened. Though we ought to maintain with good faith our engagements, if the conduct of the other party releases us, we should not refuse the release, so far as we may accept without compromitting [sic] our peace." [45] He perceived that the treaty could only be inconvenient in the future. "Hence, I want to get rid of that treaty by mutual consent, or liquidate its meaning to a treaty of definite succor, in a clearly defensive war. . . ." [46] The United States would have to permit her vessels to arm, he insisted, for "At all events our trade must have protection; for our whole mercantile capital will else be destroyed, our seamen lost, and our country involved in extreme distress." [47] There was nothing to be gained in a formal war with France. "Trade she has none — and as to territory, if we could make acquisitions they are not undesirable." [48] He conceived that the overthrow of England and the invasion of America were quite possible. The situation pointed out two objects: "1. measures of immediate defence to our Commerce, and 2. of ulterior security in the event of open Rupture." [49]

What of England, Hamilton asked? It was best to avoid alliance with her, he asserted. Mutual interest would command as much from her as a treaty. If Britain could maintain her own ground, we would

[43] Hamilton to James McHenry, March 22, 1797. *Ibid.*, 242.
[44] Hamilton to Timothy Pickering, March 22, 1797. *Ibid,*. 245-46.
[45] Hamilton to Oliver Wolcott, Nov. 22, 1796. Gibbs, *op. cit.*, I, 400.
[46] Hamilton to Theodore Sedgwick, Feb. 26, 1797. Lodge, *Works*, X, 240.
[47] Hamilton to Timothy Pickering, May 11, 1797. *Ibid.*, 246.
[48] Hamilton to James McHenry, 1798. Steiner, *op. cit.*, 292.
[49] Hamilton to James McHenry, 1798. Steiner, *The Life and Correspondence of James McHenry*, 293.

not fall prey, but if she could not a treaty would be a public bond. We took all the chances of her fall should we make a treaty with Britain and observe it. An advantageous offer of peace terms by France endeavoring to detach us from a British treaty would be difficult and dangerous to resist, he thought. "'Twill be best not to entangle." [50] The United States ought to sound Britain out as to co-operation in case of open war and furnishing the United States with naval force. Here, Hamilton had in mind the Floridas, Louisiana, and Spanish South America. "All on this side the Mississippi must be ours, including both Floridas." [51] Should French policy be to seize the Floridas and Louisiana, it was wise for the United States to take possession of them herself,

to obviate the mischief of their falling into the hands of an active foreign power, and at the same time to secure to the United States the advantage of keeping the key to the Western country. I have been long in the habit of considering the acquisition of those countries as essential to the permanency of the Union which I consider as very important to the welfare of the whole. [52]

The United States was able to avoid war and a convention was signed with France in 1800. Hamilton advised that it be ratified, for by it "our relations with France will have received a precise shape". [53] If not ratified, the ruin of the federal party would be finished and American internal tranquillity endangered. [54] A most important consequence of ratification was that future generations could say that the "federal administration steered the vessel through all the storms raised by the contentions of Europe into a peaceful and safe port". [55]

[50] *Ibid.*, 294.
[51] *Ibid.*, 295.
[52] Hamilton to Harrison Gray Otis, Jan. 26, 1799. Lodge, *Works*, X, 339.
    Hamilton made plans in 1803 for the Floridas and New Orleans. Two plans were available, he felt: (1) negotiate and endeavor to purchase; this failing, to go to war. (2) "To seize at once on the Floridas and New Orleans, and then negotiate." Since war would probably be resorted to in both instances, the second plan was best. Why? Because acquisition was easy and the preservation afterwards easy. War with France at that time was not formidable for her fleet was crippled and powerless, her treasury empty, and her resources dried up. In addition, "we might count with certainty on the aid of Great Britain with her powerful navy". "Pericles", 1803. Lodge, *Works*, VI, 334-35.
[53] Hamilton to Gouverneur Morris, Jan. 10, 1801. Lodge, *Works*, X, 410.
[54] Hamilton sought to obtain assurances from Jefferson, whose election to the Presidency was imminent, that the present system would be maintained, "especially on the cardinal articles of public credit — a navy, neutrality". Hamilton to Gouverneur Morris, Dec. 24, 1800. Lodge, *Works*, X, 400-01.
[55] Hamilton to Gouverneur Morris, Jan. 10, 1801. *Ibid.*, 411.

There was nothing in the convention contrary to the treaty with Great Britain. There were, however, features which would not be pleasant to the British cabinet, such as the principle that free ships make free goods, that the flag of warships should protect. These were points by which France was endeavoring to form hostile combinations against Britain. Allowing them in the convention expressed an unfriendly attitude toward Britain and was to be regretted. We had a right to make these stipulations and as they were supposed to be advantageous to us they were not indications of enmity. They did not give any real cause of umbrage, and considering Britain's general interests and situation, it was not probable that they would produce hostile conduct on her part.[56] Recent intelligence from Britain strengthened the argument for simple ratification, Hamilton noted. Britain stood on a precipice, for there were symptoms that her paper currency was depreciated and depreciating. The limitation of time imposed on the treaty was desirable, for perpetual peace would never exist. He said: "A war cuts the knot, and leaves us free to renew or not, to renew absolutely, or with qualifications." [57]

Hamilton reminded his fellow countrymen that:

Our conduct heretofore has gone on the ground that, though we ought not to submit to *unequivocal disgrace*, yet we ought not to be too susceptible or overcurious and nice. In this spirit we have borne a great deal, sometimes too much, from all the *belligerents*. Circumstances do not now invite to a different course. Our rapid progress to *strength will*, erelong, encourage to and warrant higher pretensions.[58]

Hamilton's attitudes and policies regarding France suggest several observations which are helpful in evaluating the British orientation of his foreign policy. The obvious conclusion to be drawn is that Hamilton would offer to France as well as to Great Britain the same official bearing. American neutrality, advantageous commercial relations, and national independence were of first importance. Should France threaten these as had Great Britain, she would be met with the same policies Hamilton designed for dealing with Britain. If France should invite mutually beneficial relations, these would receive thorough consideration by the American government, as would any such British proposals. Hamilton it seems distrusted the motives of the French more than he did the designs of the British. It may

---

[56] Hamilton to Gouverneur Morris, Dec. 24, 1800. *Ibid.*, 399-400.
[57] *Ibid.*, 410.
[58] *Ibid.*, 409.

be that Hamilton relied on the confidence pressure often demanded in dealing with Great Britain, since during the active years of his participation in government, America's future was greatly threatened by Britain. Nevertheless, Hamilton would treat with Britain and France in the same way, so long as both understood his plans for the United States.

CHAPTER VIII

THE CENTRAL THESIS

A brief review of the basic Hamiltonian themes will be helpful at this time. Hamilton insisted, first, that the United States must preserve peace to insure her growth into nationhood. It was her interest to do so. Interest was the motivation for all decisions and actions in Hamilton's estimation — it was the factor which guided national conduct. It followed that all matters concerning obligations and contracts would be evaluated on this basis.

What was the best policy for the United States to follow? Hamilton found that neutrality suited our interests at that time. Our true policy was to cultivate neutrality, for a nation could best build her strength by remaining peaceful. To operate a neutral policy, the United States would need a foreign policy adjustable to change and capable of modification. Conciliation and compromise were therefore called for. Negotiation would be the means of accomplishment, fortified always by preparation for administering American rights if negotiation failed.

Along with these fundamental themes, Hamilton developed a program for building a nation. Three ingredients were necessary: commercial intercourse, national independence, and international respect. To make these operative, it was necessary to understand the political nature of men and nations. Wars were inevitable, said Hamilton. They were the chief source of expense in government. Because of the unique position of the United States, geographically and politically, there was a hope that she might avoid wars. The United States would have to look out for her own security by avoiding war, but this did not imply complete isolation from other nations. The crucial point from which national independence and international respect would emanate was a stable economy. The most productive source of national wealth was commerce, which would involve the United States in foreign relations. Hamilton's intention then would be to look for the most beneficial associations or attachments for the commercial advantage of the United States.

America's parent and recent enemy was Hamilton's choice. The fact that this choice may have coincided with a personal preference on Hamilton's part should not bear undue weight in our evaluation. Hamilton was endowed with objective inclination in any direction which best served the ends he sought. It was from Great Britain that the United States could derive the surest, quickest and most benefit in her commercial transactions, and hence, in her revenues. In addition, the blessings were consanguine, a factor which might well aid the United States in her economic program.

The basic themes which permeate Hamilton's policy operated directly upon and interactingly with his program for building national strength via economic security. Therefore, we can not separate the consequence of one from the other, nor can we fail to recognize the interaction envisaged by Hamilton. Since commercial intercourse comprehended international relations, Hamilton was drawn to managing both wherever necessary. There is no doubt that Hamilton thought he could direct such programs in the most fruitful and effective way. He became increasingly convinced of this as he matured and aged.

The primary factor which should be recognized is that Hamilton was a nationalist. Let us look back over some of the facts to verify this statement. Hamilton's perceptiveness may be selected as perhaps his greatest gift; this perception was for the future — long range in its outlook, rather than immediate. When the Anglo-American settlement following the Revolution was received, he warned Washington of the repercussions to be expected under its stipulations. He foretold the violations both sides would cultivate and became the champion for faithful execution of its articles. Why did he take this stand? Because, he said, the United States was in no condition to force compliance with her claims, and breaches of the treaty on the American side would most likely encourage Britain to the same reaction. Moreover, if the United States set a pattern of failure to fulfill her engagements, how could she ever hope to receive the faith of other nations in future relations?

According to Hamilton, the United States was the real beneficiary by the peace treaty. Britain had given up and promised more than the new nation was required to. She had agreed to surrender the western posts, had yielded a vast tract of western territory which included one half of the Great Lakes giving the United States what Hamilton thought would be almost the whole fur trade, renounced her claim to navigation of the Mississippi, and admitted the United States into a share of the fisheries. In return, the new nation only promised not to subject British adherents in the United States to any further or future injury. Common sense alone recognized the desirable position in which the United States found herself at the end of the war.

Hamilton despaired that the United States might throw out her advantages for the mere gratification of resentments. This was sheer folly. A renewal of war with Britain was not an immediate fear, Hamilton reasoned, but Britain did remain in a position to withhold execution of features of the agreement. If Britain decided to do so, the United States could rely on nothing to force compliance. It was out of our power, a fact which the United States and the whole world knew. France was in no position to help us either, nor was it in her interest to do so. The overriding concern in Hamilton's mind was that by violating the treaty, the United States was putting in jeopardy her real interests — the frontier posts, the possession of which secured our western frontier and the fur trade, the use of the fisheries, and the hope for commercial concessions. Without these, Hamilton despaired of the American future. His practical nature allowed for complying with the required for the promise of the benefits, which in this case were extensive. It was foolhardy to blunder about and contrive to adjust stipulations which were primarily beneficial, when the continuation of the agreement was at the whim or present preoccupation of a more powerful partner.

The evident weakness of the Confederation governmental machinery and a correspondingly feeble military offense and defense, did not recommend the present schemes of the United States to Hamilton. Practical respect for facts could not fail to admit that it was in Britain's power and not in America's to determine the outcome of the treaty. Why then should the United States oblige Britain to violate further the treaty by her own discriminations, instead of sponsoring responsibility to the obligation via impeccable adherence? The reasoning of Hamilton argued for strict observance of the treaty. American interests were more surely benefited by such behavior.

Hamilton's assessment of the anaemic condition of the Confederation government accorded with the opinion of his contemporaries. The new Constitution held the promise of rectifying American governmental deficiencies and Hamilton was one of the first to adapt American policy to this new found strength. His international program did not at once adopt an aggressive tenor, nor did it ever, except in cases where pressure promoted fulfillment. His foreign policy acted in the capacity of an adjunct to the independence, security, national wealth, and international respect of the United States.

As Secretary of the Treasury Hamilton was in a position to foster his plans. Economic affluence was a critical feature of national success in any nation. The Secretary prepared programs which would promote this end, and in doing so involved himself of necessity in foreign relations. He first had to see that the United States liquidated her outstanding obligations, both politically and monetarily, or the financial security of the United States would lose respect and be dishonored.[1]

Between 1783 and 1794 American foreign relations were threatened most seriously by Great Britain. It was with Britain that our outstanding difficulties lay. American relations with Spain and the Mississippi were accessory to what we salvaged from Britain, and American relations with France had been theoretically established by the Alliance of 1778. It is true that Franco-American relations were irritated by popular favor for France in America, excited by Genet and by a question of our participation with France in her war, but not in the same likeness nor as seriously as British-American relations evidenced. With Britain it became a question of either a declaration of war or negotiation for the settlement of our problems. And, at the time these crises were in effect, Hamilton was establishing

---

[1] Hamilton's opinion of his own value in charting and attempting these programs appears to have been extremely confident. It is evident that Hamilton felt no one could do the job so well as he. He made an art of the personal act of diplomacy and seemed to experience little timidity or shyness in trespassing upon or usurping departmental provinces. He took it upon himself to express to Great Britain the official views of the United States government on several occasions. If the representations of his colleagues undermined his own designs, he seemed to feel sure his word was final and authoritative. The self-confidence and assurance Hamilton expressed in his own programs was unshakable. Hamilton apparently believed in them thoroughly. It would be hard to imagine a man taking the part of a prime contractor on a job which he did not believe in. Hamilton's actions were not those of a man who had little faith in himself or in his program. This may well account for Hamilton's concept of his right to talk with Hammond on matters outside his jurisdiction as Secretary of the Treasury, and for his effrontery in evaluating for Hammond the Secretary of State's correspondence.

his programs for American independence. Without the security of peace he could not accomplish his purpose, and America's peace was apparently threatened more certainly by Britain than by France between 1783 and 1794.

There are two known instances in which Hamilton actually conversed with representatives of the British government, that is, Major Beckwith and George Hammond. These are two excellent examples of a master diplomat at work — examples of the give and take necessary to the accomplishment of decisions and settlements between nations. Hamilton did not have much to bargain with, but much to bargain for. With the astuteness of an agile diplomat he maneuvered the United States into almost twenty years of peace, a time which allowed the United States to grow in strength and prosperity.

Beckwith came offering alliance with Great Britain should war between Britain and Spain break out. He told Hamilton that such an alliance was in the interest of all commercial nations and the United States would thus find it in her interest to join. Beckwith's offical justification for such an offer was a letter bearing only the signature "Dorchester" and no reference to the British cabinet. Hamilton noted this and did not fail to remind Beckwith that his offer seemed to be only the sentiments of Lord Dorchester. When they met a second time Hamilton took an opposite and positive attack which implied that of course Beckwith was acting officially and would not make such an offer without sanction. Beckwith was immediately placed on the defensive by this turn of conversation, for he now had to be able to prove his offer had backing. Hamilton implied that Gouveneur Morris' mission exemplified the willingness of the United States government to deal via official channels, when he noted the difference between that mission and Beckwith's.

Having made all this clear, he then proceeded to tell Beckwith what the United States was willing to allow. We were ready and interested to see that all misunderstanding between the two countries was obviated. The thought of alliance opened a wide field, he thought, and would require the specific mention of points and particulars to afford better ground for conversation. Until then, he would be unable to either raise Beckwith's expectations or repress them. Hamilton was evidently wary of Beckwith's authorization. Beckwith's fellow countryman, Temple, was also puzzled. But the contact was still interesting and need not be muzzled in case it should be a real feeler by Great Britain.

Beckwith also asked Hamilton what connection existed between Spain and the United States and how the Mississippi question was faring. One of Hamilton's policies was to keep the United States out of war, by neutrality or negotiation. What he told Beckwith respecting Spain, allowed him to operate American policy within these two objectives. There was no particular connection between Spain and the United States to his knowledge, he said, and it was public knowledge that the Mississippi question remained unsettled. As long as he indicated there was no connection between Spain and the United States, the United States would not be thought by Britain to be acting in a hostile manner toward her. In case war did erupt between Spain and Britain, since everything had been kept vague and open, the United States would be in a position to turn the war to her own benefit to settle disputes between the United States and Britain and the United States and Spain.

In the conversations with Beckwith Hamilton experimented with techniques he would find useful in talking with Hammond. These were techniques on the personal plane of suggestion, interpretation, recommendation, admonition, and consultation. By utilizing these methods we shall see that Hamilton was able to realize a degree, even if small, of progress toward his ultimate goal of American national independence.

By the time Hammond met with Hamilton in their now famous and well-known intimate conversations, Anglo-American relations were driving in two directions. The United States and Britain were intent on settling violations of the 1783 treaty and both were thinking seriously of commercial advantages, the United States hungrily and Britain thoughtfully. America eyed international trade with a jealous eye and Britain was the leading commercial nation of that day. As Hamilton noted on more than one occasion, United States economy and commerce had much to gain from trade with Britain and much to lose if we were at war with Britain directly or via association with France. The United States had always sought to establish beneficial commercial arrangements with nations, so Hamilton's drive was not new. Britain knew we were actively courting advantageous commercial relations with her. She was stringing us along on fulfillment of the treaty to gain time to develop her interests in the western country and Canada. The United States was not in a position to demand complete or even partial execution, but she could continue to dicker to retain the semblance of political intercourse. This Hamilton did in his conversations with George Hammond. It is perhaps too much to say that he gave the British just enough encouragement and enough sternness to undermine their intentions and achieved American security. In any event, the British foreign office noticed and recognized his activity, and may have been induced by his suggestions into thinking they wanted or would consider what they were not consciously planning for. An assessment of this kind is extremely difficult, for the explanations were lost to history when the characters in the events passed from life.

Hamilton's conversations with Hammond as reported earlier in the work, encourage one to think that Hamilton was guiding them and not guided by them. We have noted that Hamilton had a number of consistent themes in his policies — peace, interest, neutrality, negotiation — which were the cornerstones of his foreign relations and were designed to facilitate the completion of his national program. The revelations and disclosures he made to Hammond do not deviate from these principles. Hammond suggested to Hamilton a British mediation for fostering a quicker end to the devastations of the Indian war. Hamilton told Hammond that the United States did not wish to extend her territory but only to quell the Indians. If this could not be done by negotiation, then we would continue to prosecute the war vigorously. The United States would accept with gratitude Britain's voluntary interposition if it might help us accomplish an end to the war. He followed this with an admission that the crisis bore important relation to future American political and commercial connections with Europe. A hint was dropped that France was holding out to the United States additional advantages which would continue to favor and promote United States navigation. Then Hamilton finished by telling Hammond that he was preparing a report on American navigation and commerce which balanced commercial encouragements for America in Britain's favor. Just what had Hamilton done here? He said that we would be grateful for Britain's interposition. The crisis would, however, have important repercussions on our European connections. France was enticing us, but we had seen that Britain encouraged our trade more than France. Flattery, threat, and flattery, in that order. Britain's interest in mediation was bound to continue whether encouraged or discouraged, because her interests were served by such a policy. Encouraging it by a general sort of statement was not harmful when it gave Hamilton an opportunity to tie in commercial interests.

Hammond presented the mediation plan on several other occasions. The British did not soon give up this idea — they made a last offer during Jay's sojourn in London. Added to it later was the idea of an independent Indian nation or Indian barrier state. Hamilton and his fellow administrators refused with such force any plan which involved a cession of right or territory that an official British mediation was never accomplished. The Americans would have admitted national flaccidity had they recognized an Indian barrier state.

In the course of the conversations the questions needing negotiation between Britain and the United States were discussed. On one subject Hamilton was adamant — the western posts. These were the real source of friction to which everything else became secondary. Hamilton did not evade their importance when talking with Hammond, telling him that the surrender of the posts was really the only problem which could produce long and difficult investigation. The posts were the key to the security of western America, both territorially and commercially. If they were in American hands we would be able to avail ourselves of the fur trade, and moreover, American navigational rights on the Mississippi would be proportionately strengthened. The United States would not be induced to part with any territory acquired by the treaty he told Hammond, but she might grant British subjects the protection of the posts for the continued prosecution of the fur trade. Jefferson and Knox participated with Hamilton in the sentiment that American possession of the posts was imperative and all three agreed to consent to any conditions which Britain deemed essential to the security of her commercial or political interests, except territorial cession. The suggestions made by Hamilton and his Cabinet associates later made up part of Article three in Jay's Treaty.

The negro slave question was not really a serious problem Hamilton indicated, a viewpoint he maintained even after Jay's Treaty was promulgated. Britain's only real complaint, said Hamilton, was the subject of British creditors. This cause of complaint, he told Hammond, would be completely removed by the operation of the United States judiciary system. He readily admitted the importance of British commerce to the United States. We wanted access to the carrying trade with the West Indies. Hamilton said we would accept the restrictions and regulations Britain might require to limit the size and tonnage of vessels participating in the trade and those needed to keep us from interfering in the European trade of the British West

Indies. Hamilton's preliminary conversations with Hammond on existing difficulties between the two countries may have been influential in the final outcome of Jay's Treaty, for the treaty in its completed form gave evidence of the skeleton Hamilton designed for
Hammond.

When war between France and England broke out in 1793, Britain,
of course, was interested in the position the United States would
assume. Hammond inquired of Hamilton what the country planned
to do. In line with his consistent reliance on definite policies, Hamilton told him that he was planning to see that the United States
remained neutral. Hammond seemed to be sure that Hamilton's
declaration was believable, for the system designed by him for the
benefit of the United States would be endangered by war.

John Jay was sent as Envoy Extraordinary to Great Britain in
1794 as a last effort to avoid war. During this time Hamilton and
Hammond continued to communicate, but by 1793 and 1794 Hamilton's tone became increasingly determined and less courting. He
made Hammond feel the excitement that was spreading throughout
the United States over the continued depredations on American
shipping by Britain. Hamilton's and his country's heated temper
were reported to the home office by Hammond, so that Britain was
aware that things had come to a head.

Hammond and Hamilton had one other serious series of conversations which involved American interest in a proposed Danish-Swedish
concert against Great Britain. Hamilton's revelations to Hammond
in the course of these talks were consistent with all his policies, conforming especially to his program of neutrality. As far as he was
concerned, American attachment to such a concert would avail her
nothing. Denmark and Sweden were hardly strong enough for their
own security, let alone for helping a partner who was 4,000 miles
away. Why should the United States throw over her negotiations
with Britain, which would surely be the case should Britain know
of such a connection, when the United States had hopes of settling
her differences by treaty. It was established American policy not to
become entangled in European affairs, and Hamilton only reasserted
this when he let Hammond know we would not deviate from such
a principle. To have acted otherwise would have been to under-
estimate British intelligence, for which Hamilton retained great
respect.

The facts indicate that Hamilton betrayed little to Britain via

Beckwith and Hammond, which she did not already know or could not have found out. He gave Britain no treasonable information. He did, however, plant seeds of which some bore fruit and others remained dormant. He kept alive America's claims so that when the time came the foundation was laid for negotiating Anglo-American differences. Hamilton's designs were in part selfish and definitely nationally oriented. The success of his programs rested on the peaceful status of the United States, and, in his thinking, the future of the United States depended on the success of his programs. Even while negotiating the immediate causes of friction between the two countries, he never lost an opportunity to insert other suggestions which interested the United States. His gift for artful diplomacy was immense.

The Nootka Sound controversy threatened the security of the western country. Spain and Britain were the threats who might seduce our western settlements and jeopardize our interest in the Mississippi. Hamilton's studied opinion, when queried by Washington as to what answer should be given Lord Dorchester should he request the right of passage through United States territory, on first notice appears unusual. He recommended that we allow the passage. In doing so, he was merely conforming to the over-all rationale of his plan. He reasoned that refusal to allow Britain passage required a resolution or force to support the refusal. The mouth of the Mississippi was the key to our security. In the hand of either Britain or Spain, our security was still thwarted. Our best policy would be to avoid war. War would have to follow our refusal, because we could not enforce the refusal, or else we would have to subject ourselves to complete disgrace. War in America's condition was worse than the acquisition by another foreign power of the territories around the mouth of the Mississippi. We should therefore not refuse passage, avoiding as far as possible embroiling ourselves with Great Britain.

Refusal, Hamilton feared, would give the complexion of American indisposition toward Great Britain, which could be represented as a deviation from strict neutrality. Hamilton's strained reasoning here might well imply partiality toward Britain, but only if it is removed from the context of Hamilton's over-all plans. It must be remembered that Hamilton's national programs required peace as well as the succor of commercial revenues with Great Britain. He was offering Washington his reasons for suggesting that Britain be allowed passage. The tenor of these suggestions would transfer the importance of his message and probably influence the decision to be made. If the United States aggravated Britain over an issue which placed us at no greater disadvantage with her than already existed, Hamilton's greater plans would suffer. The partiality expressed in Hamilton's reasoning was more a partiality for his own programs than for Great Britain.

If we did not throw any impediment in Britain's way, good humor might beget a greater moderation from her, and concessions could be made by her as the price of our future neutrality. The United States had more urgent reason to differ with Spain than with Britain. Once the question of the detention of the western posts was settled, there was no necessary source of future collision with Britain. America's true policy was to cultivate neutrality, Hamilton said, until we had the strength to change the scene as we wished. Hamilton's choice was between two evils, and in his estimation he singled out the lesser. The content of his decision illustrates once again themes of his plan — peace and neutrality.

Hamilton took an active part in the American policy emanating from the declaration of war by France on all of Europe. There was considerable sentimental attachment in the United States for France, and our obligations by the Alliance of 1778 foretold a request for our participation on her side in her war. Hamilton's main themes in this event were compliant with those already set forth: avoid involvement in war by maintaining neutrality, so that the most lucrative source of national wealth — revenue and/or America's interest — would not be disrupted. Any threat to America's commercial relations or the security of her revenue elicited a rebuttal from Hamilton based on the national interest. Since, according to Hamilton, the way of securing a stable nation and government was by economic means, he was obliged to evaluate every event in this light. With this central economic thesis evolved the Hamiltonian concepts of peace, neutrality, and negotiation in diplomacy.

The United States was tied by treaty to France, and presumably obliged to come to her aid upon request. How could we circumvent or disallow this obligation? Hamilton found the answer in his concept of obligation, which formed the theoretical basis for our right to remain neutral. The legal argument was simple. Our treaty was for purposes of defense and French actions were offensive; we were absolved by virtue of her offensive war from participating in it. We had agreed to come to her defense were she attacked, but France had declared war on almost all of Europe. Hamilton's commercial policies were threatened by war, but there was more than this to be considered. Spain and Britain were on both our flanks and the Indians were under their influence. We had a long sea coast and no navy to defend it. With the whole maritime force of Europe against us and with only a four million population, a more unequal contest could not be imagined. Simple motives of self-preservation and interest induced the United States to remain neutral.

Anglo-American relations seemed to be quickly moving toward war as the only solution of their differences in 1793 and 1794. Hamilton's programs would have been defeated in their aim had war opened. War was costly both politically and financially, nationally and internationally. We could be disgraced in war in the eyes of the world and suffer loss of pride and face. War with Britain would hurt us more than it would hurt her. Britain's credit and commerce were still very strong and it was not likely that war would arrest her career. American prosperity would be interrupted and our astonishing growth stunted. If we considered the naval superiority of French enemies, there could be no doubt but that American commerce would be annihilated by war. Our agriculture and industry would receive deep wounds. Nine-tenths of America's revenues were derived from commercial duties, Hamilton said, and no other substitute could be found except in the imposition of heavy taxes on the people. In the past Americans had not supported taxation, so that source could not be considered dependable. The national wealth of the nation depended upon revenues from commercial enterprises, and to Hamilton a stable national wealth meant independence and international respect.

Hamilton volunteered his thoughts and recommendations to Washington on the matter of war with Great Britain. The nation was acting more in anger and under the influence of perverse passions than from cool calculations of interest. The people were not of one voice in calling for war, he said, and if the government should adopt war as a policy when another way may have been possible, a deep and extensive dissatisfaction with the conduct of the government would develop. A loss of confidence in the government could prove to be the threshold of disorganization and anarchy. He thought it unlikely that Britain would submit to our demands when faced with coercion preceded by acts of reprisal. Britain was fortified with alliances of the greatest part of Europe. She would have to renounce her pride and dignity to succumb to American protestations, which no nation of Britain's stature would consider doing, and especially for a nation which had been her colony only a short time before. American plans for sequestering British debts and cutting off all commercial intercourse with Britain tended to produce war. In addition, such measures had a malignant influence on public and mercantile credit. The United States would have to enforce a complete embargo before we could distress Britain seriously, but to do so we would be depriving ourselves of a supply which was absolutely necessary to us in peacetime and more necessary in wartime — a supply for which there was no substitute elsewhere. America's revenue would receive a serious blow, and bring the Treasury to a complete stoppage, cutting up credit by the roots. The consequences, Hamilton felt, of a sudden disturbance of American trade were incalculable.

We can see in Hamilton's evaluation of the effects a British-American war would have upon American revenues, an excellent summary of his ever present attention to the preservation of American commerce. Hamilton's absorption with peace and trade should never be out of the mind of the reader, as its pertinence to the study is primary. Without peace and trade Hamilton's diplomacy and its British orientation lose their real meaning. All too often the tendency in historical interpretation is to generalization from the small or incidental, losing sight of the big picture. If Hamilton's foreign policy is to be understood in its real intent, we must avoid any such suggestions.

War, Hamilton insisted, was not yet necessary; there was room for negotiation. The United States must not make the mistake of overrating herself and underrating Great Britain. He recommended that we prepare for negotiations by preparing for war — to be in a condition to defend ourselves and annoy any who atttacked us was the best method of securing our peace.

John Jay was sent to Great Britan as America's chief negotiator. He was a close associate of Hamilton's and had received Hamilton's recommendation and support for the appointment. Hamilton wrote for Jay, an accompanying letter to the official instructions, which best presents his intentions for a treaty. It should not be forgotten that his primary concern was preserving the peace in America's own interest, but once it was decided that the United States would negotiate without self-imposed obstructions, Hamilton's practical side took the lead. He told Jay to demand a substantial indemnification for

American shipping losses, but not a complete or absolute indemnification. If a solid arrangement regarding the unexecuted portions of the peace treaty could be effected, the indemnification question should be managed with less rigor. And, finally, if a truly beneficial commercial treaty including trading privileges in the West Indies, were established, then the indemnification problem should be dealt with even more laxly. In such a case, the government could satisfy its own citizens for their losses, he thought. Hamilton's optimism in expecting to gain commercial privileges from Great Britain was based on his convictions that America was important to Britain in a commercial sense. American articles were essential to Britain for her subsistence, her manufactures, and her revenues, was his viewpoint. No other nation rivaled America as a consumer of British exports, and we would continue to increase as consumers even though we were building our own industries, for the supply would not keep up with the demand. These facts were undeniable proof that the United States had something to bargain with and for, Hamilton claimed.

The Mississippi question was even included in Hamilton's few observations to Jay. Navigation of the Mississippi was of immense importance to the United States; British interest in the river was not wanting. If we promised Britain participation in the navigation and a treaty of commerce, she might grant us recognition of our rights to the Mississippi, which would reinforce America's claims there. Jay would have to act with prudence on this subject, however, for our negotiations with Spain were showing signs of bearing fruit.

Upon reading Hamilton's instructions for Jay and his additional observations, one reflection seems to stand out. Once negotiation was allowed between the two countries, Hamilton seemed to feel that war was not so serious a threat. His attention was immediately directed towards establishing arrangements which would benefit the United States beyond merely settling the difficulties arising out of Britain's neutral shipping policies and violations of the 1783 peace settlement. His interest was in seeing how much could be gotten for the United States, not in submitting our claims to Britain's judgment. Britain had much to offer the United States in Hamilton's evaluation, and his opportunity to acquire for America some of the fortunes Great Britain basked in came in the Jay negotiations. Since 1789 he had been planting seeds for national and foreign fruition, all directed toward national independence and security. It was Britain who happened to still retain our posts, who was the leading commercial dissatisfaction to France, he thought. While he would not omit any measure which he thought for the national interest because a foreign power might dislike it, Hamilton still thought it wise not to do any act giving a reasonable cause for dissatisfaction. The eighteenth article, involving contraband, he feared could become the pretext of abuses on the side of Britain and complaint by France. The article allowing us entry into the British East Indies was immensely valuable, he thought, for it made a right what we had enjoyed before only by sufferance. The remaining articles concerned such matters as most-favored-nation rights, and the right to search and seize neutral ships, which were features included in most commercial treaties. In Hamilton's studied opinion the British had given the United States greater advantages in her colonies than had any other nation having colonies. There was no equivalent in any of our other treaties for the advantages Britain had given us in the British East Indies. We also had gained free entrance to Canadian commerce.

The treaty did not change our footing with France nor would it hinder our making a more beneficial treaty with her. The United States would have been foolish indeed, Hamilton stated, had she refused to negotiate with Britain, which it was in her interest to do, because of a possibility that France might make a better bargain. All France had offered was that the United States become parties to her war. By resorting to negotiation to solve our differences with Britain, the United States had assumed an august and respectable position, Hamilton concluded. Even Europe was struck by our dignified moderation, and the character of the American government and nation had acquired a new elevation in world opinion.

Great advances for the United States had been made possible by the Jay's treaty: peace was preserved, the posts surrendered, American commerce continued to proceed with success, and agriculture flourished. Peace would work its optimistic good for the next twenty years as Hamilton had planned, so that by the time war broke out in 1812 the United States was better able to represent herself against a formidable enemy. Commerce could continue to develop and with it would come the rewards of revenue, so vital in Hamilton's program for the establishment of the United States among nations.

Hamilton's unofficial and advisory participation in the crisis with France following Jay's Treaty is important to this study and analysis. Without the balance of this knowledge, the tendency would be to say that Hamilton was biased in favor of Great Britain. In fact, however, Hamilton wanted to rely on the same course of action with France as the United States had with Great Britain. He distrusted French motives, which he saw as primarily motivated by self-interest. There was nothing against interest, but it did not require obligation. As far as he was concerned, France had become our ally only to satisfy her own interests. If she had not seen advantage in alliance, she would not have allowed it. He disliked comparisons of the French and American Revolutions. He used the example of France and our alliance as a warning not to overrate foreign friendships, because underlying every feature of any relationship was interest. France was our boasted friend and benefactress, but she participated in abridging neutral rights which hurt American commerce. Hamilton saw French policy in this instance as designed to ruin British commerce, excusing the actions by charging them to the account of Jay's Treaty. The United States had not allowed Britain to do as France was doing. France led all nations in the violation of neutral rights. She was using Jay's Treaty as the excuse for continuing her depredations on neutral commerce.

Hamilton recommended that France be appealed to as we had to Britain, and this failing, we should defend our commerce and independence. The situation with France was as serious as any America had faced, Hamilton told Washington. He seemed to doubt that war could be avoided.[2] His proposals for negotiation with active preparation for war, exactly resemble those he developed for dealing with Great Britain. Peace was vital; he expected the ultimate estimation of the merit of all America's past measures would depend on the final preservation of peace.

Hamilton suggested that an envoy extraordinary be sent to France to adjust our differences amicably, while at home we should take vigorous and comprehensive measures for defense. Hamilton thought the time ready for the United States to escape from the French Alliance, as its future operation was against America's interest. The

---

[2] During the French crisis between 1789 and 1800, while Hamilton was recommending the same official approach for France which he had used on Great Britain, he was actively supporting preparations for war. He spent these years reorganizing the American military machinery. The intensity with which he dedicated his efforts to this employment may suggest that Hamilton envisaged war or the use of force at some time. War with France implied a full scale American invasion of the French mainland which was, of course, impractical and impossible. Perhaps the military force was to be used in the Western Hemisphere, since there are evidences of Hamilton's correspondence with Miranda.

treaty would be inconvenient in the future, he thought. It would need to be changed or else gotten rid of. The United States could gain little if anything in a formal war with France: she had no trade to offer and the territories in her possession were desirable but not easily obtained. Since Hamilton's French policies so resemble his British ones, it is hard to accuse him of showing partiality towards Britain at the expense of France. At the time of his most active participation in government, the United States was most deeply involved with Britain. Surely, he would have devoted his energies to solving those problems before attacking less important ones. And, when similar ones arose with another power, he impartially meted out the same recommendations.

Of what value has this study been, we might ask? Its major interest has been to place Alexander Hamilton in the respected position of a diplomatic statesman in American history, which he well deserves. As a practical politician and diplomatist he was unequalled in his day, among those in a position to guide American foreign policy. The consistency with which he pursued his goals persisted throughout the period of this study. With the national interest as his guide, and peace, neutrality, and negotiation as his tools, Hamilton directed the United States into international commerce, national independence and international respect. Using the discipline of decision-making to study Hamiltonian decisions, the preferences on which he based his choices were the themes just mentioned. It has been seen that he very probably relied for these upon principles gleaned from the Greek and Roman classics. The resemblance between them and his decisions and rationales were remarkably similar. Hamiltonian leadership is undeniable; it rarely lacked assurance or aplomb. The major strength of his leadership was that it had goals and direction. This aided the decision-making process. The national interest was the core from which each decisional choice drew its preference.

In the art of diplomacy Hamilton excelled. He would be acquaintance to all, but friend to none, as America's interests dictated. He courted those from whom America could benefit the most. From the rest he sought to keep America aloof, away from their entanglement. He would count on no favors; self-interest was the guiding factor among all nations, no less than of the United States. America's interest was the rationalization for each of his decisions. The picture of a spiral mentioned in the opening chapter of this study wondered if Hamilton's policies would be derived from the national interest or from the hope for an international community of utopia. The answer seems evidently that the national interest was the motivating factor in his rationale, and since the national interest was best served by courting Great Britain, Hamilton did so.

The dynamics of Hamiltonian diplomacy suggest one more thought. What is their place in modern diplomacy? Hamilton's diplomatic reasoning and argument, by virtue of the message they bear, are adaptable to the national and international politics of today and tomorrow. Hamilton taught the United States that a hierarchy of interests must be determined, at the base of which should be found the national interest. This, to Hamilton, was the purpose of diplomacy. A compromise between rivalries was more profitable in the long run than the complete destruction of the rival, especially if the rival were the United States, Hamilton told his countrymen. He warned that a nation which set goals it had not the power to attain faced the risk of war. Such a policy dissipated a nation's strength, leaving it too weak to deter a hostile challenge. The assessment of another nation's power was vital, for to overrate or underrate it could be to invite the end of peace.

Hamilton taught America another important lesson which is applicable to today's diplomacy. Nations wishing to pursue intelligent and peaceful foreign policies should never cease to evaluate objectives, their own and those of other nations. If American objectives were not compatible with another nation's, the United States had to determine how vital its own objectives were. In evaluating the American national interest, the United States would also need to determine how important another nation's objectives were to its own national interest. With this in mind and through diplomatic bargaining and compromise, Hamilton would seek a way by which American interests could be reconciled with the interests of another nation.

Hamiltonian diplomacy sought to choose the appropriate means for pursuing America's national interest. These were, we have seen: persuasion, compromise, and threat of force, all of which are the essence of diplomacy in the modern world. The art of diplomacy is knowing when to put the right emphasis on each of these three means. Hamilton gave the United States valuable lessons in this art.

Finally, the use of propaganda by Hamilton deserves mention. Hamilton learned very early the important lesson, which the modern world has learned equally well, that no policy could succeed unless it had national opinion behind it. Before, during, and after almost every policy move, Hamilton appealed to the American public. His propaganda was essentially persuasive in its intent, seeking to gain the support of the people. Propaganda as a technique has grown into a separate discipline in the modern world, and its place in diplomacy and diplomatic theory is almost beyond evaluation.

As one of America's leading economic and administrative statesmen Hamilton has made his place in American history. With this study Hamilton emerges in yet another area, that of a diplomatic theorist and technician. The very practical Hamiltonian foreign policy may perhaps be his greatest legacy to future American statesmen.

BIBLIOGRAPHY

Adams, Charles Francis (ed.), *The Works of John Adams* (Boston, Little, Brown and Company, 1853). 10 vols.

Adams, James Truslow (ed.), *Hamiltonian Principles, Extracts from the Writings of Alexander Hamilton* (Boston, Little, Brown and Company, 1928).

Aly, Bower, *The Rhetoric of Alexander Hamilton* (New York, Columbia University Press, 1941).

American State Papers, *Foreign Relations: Documents, Legislative and Executive, of the Congress of the United States, from the first Session of the first to the third Session of the thirteenth Congress, inclusive: Commencing March 3, 1789, and ending March 3, 1815* (Washington, Gales and Seaton, 1832), vol. 1.

Aristotle, *On Man in the Universe: Metaphysics, Parts of Animals, Ethics, Politics, Poetics* (New York, Walter J. Black, Incorporated, 1943).

Aron, Raymond, "The Quest for a Philosophy of Foreign Affairs", *Revue Française de Science Politique*, III (January-March, 1953), 77.

Atherton, Gertrude Franklin, *The Conqueror, Being the True and Romantic Story of Alexander Hamilton* (New York, Grosset and Dunlap, 1902).

Ballagh, James Curtis (ed.), *The Letters of Richard Henry Lee* (New York, The MacMillan Company, 1914), 2 vols.

Burnett, Edmund C. (ed.), *Letters of Members of the Continental Congress* (Washington, Carnegie Institution, 1921-1936), 8 vols.

Butterfield, L. H. (ed.), *Letters of Benjamin Rush* (Princeton, Princeton University Press, 1951), 2 vols.

Cicero, *The Basic Works of Cicero* (New York, Random House, 1951).

Conway, Moncure Daniel, *Omitted Chapters of History Disclosed in the Life and Letters of Edmund Randolph* (New York, G. P. Putnam's Sons, 1888).

Culbertson, William S., *Alexander Hamilton, An Essay* (New Haven, Yale University Press, 1911).

Demosthenes, *The Crown, the Philippics and Ten Other Orations of Demosthenes* (New York, E. P. Dutton and Company, 1923).

Donnan, Elizabeth (ed.), *Papers of James A. Bayard, 1796-1815.* Annual Reports of the American Historical Association for the Year 1913 (Washington, United States Government Printing Office, 1915).

Ellis, Ivan Cheever, "A Study of the Influence of Alexander Hamilton on George Washington", Unpublished Ph.D. dissertation, University of Southern California, 1956.

Fitzpatrick, John C. (ed.), *The Diaries of George Washington* (Boston, Houghton Mifflin Company, 1925), 4 vols.

——, *The Writings of George Washington* (Washington, United States Government Printing Office, 1931-1944), 39 vols.

Ford, Paul Leicester (ed.), *Pamphlets on the Constitution of the United States, Published during Its Discussion by the People 1787-1788* (Brooklyn, 1888).

——, *Letters of William Vans Murray to John Quincy Adams, 1797-1803*. Annual Reports of the American Historical Association for the Year 1912 (Washington, United States Government Printing Office, 1914).

——, *Writing of John Quincy Adams* (New York, The MacMillan Company, 1913), Vol. 1.

Gibbs, George (ed.), *Memoirs of the Administrations of Washington and John Adams, edited from the papers of Oliver Wolcott, Secretary of the Treasury* (New York, William Van Norden, 1846), 2 vols.

Hamilton, Alexander, *The Papers of Alexander Hamilton* (Washington, Library of Congress, 1915), Series I: 80 vols. Series II: 24 vols.

Hamilton, Allan McLane, *The Intimate Life of Alexander Hamilton* (New York, Charles Scribner's Sons, 1911).

Hamilton, John C., *History of the Republic of the United States of America, as Traced in the Writings of Alexander Hamilton and of his Contemporaries* (Philadelphia, J. B. Lippincott and Company, 1864), 7 vols.

——, (ed.), *The Works of Alexander Hamilton* (New York, Charles S. Francis and Company, 1860), 7 vols.

Hamilton, Stanislaus Murray (ed.), *The Writings of James Monroe* (New York, G. P. Putnam's Sons, 1898).

Hayes, Carlton, *Essays on Nationalism* (New York, The MacMillan Company, 1926).

Hunt, Gaillard (ed.), *Journals of the Continental Congress, 1774-1789* (Washington, United States Government Printing Office), 34 vols.

Johnston, Henry P. (ed.), *The Correspondence and Public Papers of John Jay* (New York, G. P. Putnam's Sons, 1891), 4 vols.

Knopf, Richard C. (ed.), *Anthony Wayne, a Name in Arms: The Wayne-Knox-Pickering-McHenry Correspondence* (Pittsburgh, University of Pittsburgh Press, 1960).

Kohn, Hans, *Nationalism: Its Meaning and History* (Princeton, C. Van Nostrand Company, 1955).

Letters of Phineas Bond, British Consul at Philadelphia, to the Foreign Office of Great Britain, 1790-1794. Annual Report of the American Historical Association for the Year 1897 (Washington, United States Government Printing Office, 1898).

Lipscomb, Andrew A. (ed.), *Writings of Thomas Jefferson* (Washington, United States Government Printing Office, 1905).

Lodge, Henry Cabot (ed.), *The Federalist, A Commentary on the Constitution of the United States* (New York, G. P. Putnam's Sons, 1882).

Lodge, Henry Cabot, *The Works of Alexander Hamilton* (New York, G. P. Putnam's Sons, 1904), 12 vols.

Lycan, Gilbert Lester, "The Foreign Policy of Alexander Hamilton", Unpublished Ph.D. dissertation. Yale University, 1942.

McKee, Samuel Fr. (ed.), *Papers on Public Credit, Commerce and Finance by Alexander Hamilton* (New York, Columbia University Press, 1934).

Mayo, Bernard (ed.), *Instructions to the British Ministers to the United States 1791-1812*. Annual Reports of the American Historical Association for the Year 1936 (Washington, United States Government Printing Office, 1941), Vol. 3.

Mitchell, Broadus, *Alexander Hamilton, Youth to Maturity, 1755-1788*.

——, *Heritage from Hamilton* (New York, Columbia University Press, 1957).

Morris, Anne Cary (ed.) *The Diary and Letters of Gouverneur Morris* (New York, Charles Scribner's Sons, 1888), 2 vols.

Morse, John T., *The Life of Alexander Hamilton* (Boston, Little, Brown, and Company, 1882).

Oliver, Frederick Scott., *Alexander Hamilton, An Essay on American Union* (New York, G. P. Putnam's Sons, 1923).

Prescott, Frederick C., *Alexander Hamilton and Thomas Jefferson* (New York, American Book Company, 1934).

Public Record Office, *Foreign Office:* Series 4 and 5 (Washington, Library of Congress Photostats).

Smucker, Samuel M., *The Life and Times of Alexander Hamilton* (Boston, L. P. Corwin and Company, 1857).

Snyder, Richard, H. W. Bruck, and Burton Sapin, *Decision-Making as an Approach to the Study of International Politics* (Princeton, Princeton University Press, 1954).

Steiner, Bernard C. (ed.), *The Life and Correspondence of James McHenry* (Cleveland, The Burrows Brothers Company, 1907).

Syrett, Harold C. (ed.), *The Papers of Alexander Hamilton* (New York, Columbia University Press, 1961), 4 vols. to date.

Thucydides, *The Complete Writings of Thucydides: The Peloponnesian War* (New York, Random House, 1934).

Turner, Frederick J. (ed.), *Correspondence of French Ministers to the United States 1791-1797*. Annual Report of the American Historical Association for the Year 1903 (Washington, United States Government Printing Office, 1904), vol. 2.

Vandenberg, Arthur Hendrick, *The Greatest American, Alexander Hamilton* (New York, G. P. Putnam's Sons, 1921).